Dan Ri...

Bengal Cats

Everything About Purchase, Care, Nutrition,

Breeding, Health Care, and Behavior

With 38 Color Photographs

Illustrations by Michele Earle-Bridges

BARRON'S

About the Author:

Dan Rice is a veterinarian who spent his professional career caring for the health of pets. His home and practice were in the Colorado Rocky Mountains until retirement. He now lives in Sun City, Arizona with Marilyn, his wife and alter ego of 40 years. While in practice, Dr. Rice wrote newspaper columns and journal articles. He is now pursuing his writing avocation of many years, and is presently preparing a collection of animal short stories for publication. In his heart, as in his practice, there has always been a special place for cats.

Photo Credits:

Barbara Andrews: page 17; Pat Eibs: back cover, page 73; Karin Donoyan: page 25; June Franklin: page 89; Catherine Glickman: page 13; Leslie Hall: pages 24, 37 (top), 48, 53, 69, 77; Gene Johnson: pages 8 (bottom), 84; Rob Kwolek: inside front cover, inside back cover; Jane Lee: page 36; Jean Mill: pages 5, 9, 37 (bottom), 45, 49, 65, 72; Terri Pattison: front cover, pages 29, 56, 57, 64, 68, 88; Joy Peel: pages 12, 76, 85; Dan Rice: pages 28, 33; Judith Strom: pages 8 (bottom), 16, 25, 32, 44, 52, 80

Page 55: the breed standard for the Bengal Cat is reprinted by permission of The International Cat Association (TICA).

All inquiries should be addressed to:
Barron's Educational Series, Inc.
250 Wireless Boulevard
Hauppauge, NY 11788

International Standard Book No. 0-8120-9243-0

Library of Congress Catalog Card No. 95-13528

Library of Congress Cataloging-in-Publication Data
Rice, Dan, 1933–
    Bengal Cats : everything about purchase, care, nutrition, breeding, health care, and behavior / Dan Rice ; drawings by Michele Earle-Bridges.
        p.   cm.—(A Complete pet owner's manual)
    Includes bibliographical references (p.) and index.
    ISBN 0-8120-9243-0
    1. Bengal cat. I. Title. II. Series.
SF449.B45R535 1995
636.8′26—dc20   95-13528
                                                      CIP

Printed in Hong Kong

14 13 12 11 10 9 8 7 6 5

Important Note:
When you handle cats, you may sometimes get scratched or bitten. If this happens, have a doctor treat the injuries immediately.

Make sure your cat receives all the necessary shots and dewormings, otherwise serious danger to the animal and to human health may arise. A few diseases and parasites can be communicated to humans. If your cat shows any signs of illness, you should definitely consult a veterinarian. If you are worried about your own health, see your doctor and tell him or her that you have cats.

Some people have allergic reactions to cats. If you think you might be allergic, see your doctor before you get a cat.

It is possible for a cat to cause damage to someone else's property and even to cause accidents. For your own protection you should make sure your insurance covers such eventualities, and you should definitely have liability insurance.

Contents

Preface

The important Bengal historical information contained in this book was made possible by the generous assistance that I received from Jean Sugden Mill. Her infectious fascination with Bengal cats was quickly transmitted to the Rice family! Her personal contributions, criticism, and suggestions allowed me to get this book off the ground. With my sincere gratitude I dedicate this volume to my friend Jean.

Catherine Glickman, an attorney and devoted Bengal breeder, was invaluable in proofreading and advising me as the book developed.

I would be amiss if I did not thank the Bengal breeders who contributed their pictures, advice, and information. Among them are Gene Johnson, Joy Peel, Terri Pattison, Leslie Hall, Karin Donoyan, Jane Lee, Barbara Andrews, and others who answered my questionnaires. My colleagues, the zoo veterinarians and feline practitioners who allowed me to use their libraries and pick their brains, were essential contributors as well, and a special thanks to Phil Shanker, D.V.M. for his help. Also deserving recognition are Leslie Bowers and the TICA staff who were very accommodating.

Dan Rice

Introduction to the Bengal

Historical Notes on the Cat

Cats have been a part of human cultures since history was first recorded. They occupied an important place in families of the ruling classes of ancient Egypt where they were worshipped by and enshrined with the pharaohs' families. The Egyptian goddess of light and music, depicted as a cat-headed figure, was considered the protector of all cats. A penalty of death was imposed upon anyone who killed a cat, either purposefully or accidentally. Egyptian aristocrats took their cats seriously!

Cats are remarkable creatures whose habits and characteristics caused them to reign in honor in one era and to be detested and shunned in another. During the Middle and Dark Ages of Europe, cats regained prominence in human society. Only at that time, they were hated and feared. They

Painting inside Egyptian tomb showing spotted cat with bird.

were considered to be supernatural companions of witches and demons, and to see a black cat was sure to bring bad luck. Cats represented evil in the culture of those days, and they were sometimes executed in formal rites. In the unlettered society of medieval Europe, there were many reasons for apprehension and fear of cats.

Being nocturnal animals, cats are often perceived as shadows in the night, seeming to appear and disappear like specters on their soft and silent footpads. Their athletic ability allows them to effortlessly jump great heights and vanish like magic over a fence or onto a rooftop. The vibrissae (tactile hairs) on each side of their muzzles act as "feelers" that measure the size of a space before they enter it. They move quickly and silently through tiny apertures, in a phantom-like manner. They possess little if any body odor and they bury their excretions, making their lives even more secretive and mysterious. They are accomplished hunters and are fastidious in their grooming habits, appearing sleek and shiny, even when the humans around them are poorly fed and clothed. It is little wonder that the untutored masses considered them supernatural beings.

Survival of *Felis catus*

The members of the genus *Felis* are solitary hunters and do not establish packs or prides. In that regard, they resemble their cousins the leopards and tigers more closely than the lions and cheetahs who make up the other genera of the Felidae family. The lack of dependency on others may contribute to the survival of *Felis* in the wild.

A farm cat society in a rural, uncontrolled environment usually contains a dominant tom who is physically superior to all others. He will try to maintain that superiority by destroying male kittens as soon as they are born and he

will attack and drive off other males of breeding age who enter his territory. The queens in his bailiwick, however, depend on the tom only for mating to propagate the species. Individual female cats effectively accept the responsibility for hunting and providing for their kittens.

Unfortunately, that survival instinct is not all good. Well-meaning human families obtain feline pets; then for various reasons, they fail to care for them properly. They become stray and abandoned cats that are pests in cities and suburbia. Unchecked diseases in stray cat populations maintain reservoirs of infection for family pets. Pounds and shelters are overwhelmed by the thousands of abandoned cats and untold numbers of them are humanely destroyed annually in the United States.

Stray cats are the innocent victims, not the criminals. They suffer and die from diseases and injuries that go untreated. The country's appalling stray cat dilemma can only be solved by well-informed people who are willing to take full responsibility for their cats.

As a species, cats were probably among the last animals to be domesticated by man. Perhaps that is because of their extreme intelligence, independence, and physical agility. It is said that people fall into one of two categories: ailurophiles (cat lovers) and ailurophobes (those who fear or hate cats)—few people have no opinions about the species. Fortunately, the ailurophiles are gaining ground in the United States and in many European countries. Among family pets in the United States today, cats are more populous than dogs.

Unlike the dog and most other domesticated species of mammals, cats adapt to human cultures primarily for the mutual benefits of such a relationship. Their domestication probably began when they moved their dens

Classification of the Asian Leopard Cat

ORDER: **Carnivora**

   FAMILY: **Felidae**

      GENUS: **Acinonyx** (cheetah)

             Panthera (lion, tiger, leopard)

             Felis (house cat, leopard cat, golden cat, ocelot, margay, lynx, caracal, mountain lion, jaguarundi, pampas cat, Andean cat, Palla's cat, clouded leopard, marbled cat, serval, fishing cat, flat-headed cat)

close to human encampments to feed upon small rodents that were attracted to granaries and kitchens. Meat scraps under dining tables may have influenced them to enter human dwellings and share their victuals when hunting was poor. When householders discovered the cats' uncanny ability to control rodent populations in their homes and storehouses, a mutually beneficial association was begun.

Most mammals apparently developed trust and dependency on humans and accepted their leadership before they became domesticated. A horse, dog, or even a wolf will follow and serve a human if that human is established as the dominant (alpha) member of their society. In early days, and perhaps even today, submission to human leadership is not the determining factor in the relationship between cats and humans. Although they have a pecking order, cats do not embrace the idea of following any leader, not even another cat.

In some cases of long-term, closely controlled cat breeding programs, cats may submit to a human as the leader of their family. In those cases, that submission is probably related to the human's selection of breeding animals, neutering all that do not meet strict standards. As certain personalities and characteristics are chosen and perpetuated by selective breeding, eventually an individual breed may become dependent upon

humans. In which case, someday humans may enjoy the total trust and discipleship of a cat breed. Considering the vast and diverse genetic pool of mixed-breed cats in the country, it is doubtful that such a relationship will ever exist between humans and cats as a species.

No doubt all domestic breeds of cats can trace their origin to feral ancestors. Certainly small, wild cats that closely resemble the common house cat can be found throughout much of the eastern world. One principal difference between all other domestic cats and the Bengal is its proximity to its wild ancestor.

Bengal Ancestry

The Bengal cat of this book is a domesticated house cat. It is an even-tempered, gentle, affectionate, and playful family pet. The name of the breed, Bengal, has no relationship to the Bengal tiger. The domestic Bengal derived its name from the species name of its wild ancestor, *Felis bengalensis*, an Asian leopard cat. The Bengal cat that is discussed in detail in the following chapters is four or more generations removed from that wild species. Its appearance is similar to the Asian leopard cat, and its genetic makeup contains a contribution from that wild cat species. *Its temperament, however, is purely domestic.* The purposeful production of a domestic breed from a wild

7

species was a difficult and time-consuming task. The goal in developing the domestic Bengal cat breed was to preserve a strong physical resemblance to its beautiful wild ancestor. At the same time, the new domestic breed was designed to be a pleasant and trustworthy family companion.

Production of the Bengal breed required diluting and virtually eliminating the timid, reclusive, and untamable characteristics inherent in the wild leopard cat species. That genetic dilution has been done by experts who have carefully crossbred the Asian leopard cat with certain domestic cats. As with any new breed of cats, a great deal of curiosity exists about the Bengal. The questions most frequently asked relate to the breed characteristics, and to the authenticity of its wild origin. Naturally, many prospective Bengal owners want to know more about the breed's ancestral wild Asian leopard cat.

Felis bengalensis

Taxonomists generally agree on the genus name *Felis* and the species name *catus* for the common domestic house cat. Some zoologists consider each of the other 16 cats also listed

Closeup of cat in the painting on page 5.

under the genus *Felis* as separate species, and give each a distinctive species name. Other taxonomists group all of the small Asian leopard cats under the genus *Felis* and species *bengalensis.* They list the various wild Asian cats as subspecies or varieties of the species *bengalensis.*

The modern domestic Bengal cat retains the beauty of its wild ancestor.

Bengalensis refers to the Bengal region of India.

In addition to those found in India, various other Asian leopard cat sub-species were used to produce the domestic Bengal breed, some of which were indigenous to Malaysia and Thailand. Asian leopard cat here refers to any of the species, sub-species, or varieties of small, wild, spotted Asian cats that are genetically compatible with *F. catus.* All leopard cats are wild, and leopard cats played a vital role in the development of the domestic Bengal breed.

Description of the Asian Leopard Cat

Asian leopard cats are wild animals with many of the traits of other wild felines. As other wild animals, leopard cats' instinctive, genetically wired traits surface as they mature. A newborn Asian leopard kitten that is taken from its dam at birth, nursed by a domestic cat, and handled daily by a human, may temporarily appear to bond to its human counterpart. It may accept han-dling, petting, and playing with humans for several months; then it grows up.

No matter how Asian leopard cats are raised, when sexually mature, they are not tame or domesticated. They don't spend the evening purring con-tentedly on your lap. They are solitary, nocturnal, wild animals that are shy and reclusive, and will rarely allow han-dling or touching by a human. They instinctively resent being "cornered," and may become aggressively defen-sive when protecting their young. Like other wild animals, they usually have no interest in human companionship, and receive no pleasure from petting.

Like most wild felines, they will adapt to zoolike surroundings, where they can hide or pace, depending on their moods. They will spray urine on walls and bedding, defecate from high perches, and urinate or defecate in their

drinking water. Observers and students of this species agree that although the leopard cat is small in size by compari-son to the tiger, lion, leopard, and cougar, it is probably less tamable.

The leopard cats' habitat extends throughout Asia, including the main-land and the island countries. Some of the leopard cat varieties have their own descriptive names that are related to the particular region or country in which they occur. Other subspecies have common names that describe their habits, such as "the fishing cat." Physically descriptive common names such as "rusty spotted cat" or "flat-headed cat" are used to identify other subspecies. In some regions of Asia, leopard cats are nearly extinct, and many species are considered endan-gered or threatened.

The intensity of coat colors of Asian leopard cats are darkest in the warmer regions and lightest in the cool cli-mates of the continent. Background coat colors vary from light, hazy blue-gray or tan to dark brown or dark gray, with shades of yellow and green occur-ring in some. All share the horizontally aligned or random contrasting spots that are characteristic of the species. Some have spots that resemble

Male Asian leopard cat Cameo Keepsake *owned by Jean Mill.*

An Asian leopard cat.

rosettes, whereas others have solid colored spots. Some have triangular shaped spots, others are round. The ocelli, which is a very noticeable white spot on the back of their dark colored ears, is common to all leopard cats. Black spots above the eyes, black tail tip, spotted, light-colored bellies, and black and white stripes on their faces are also prevalent markings.

The general body structure of *Felis bengalensis* is similar to that of domestic felines. Some subspecies are a bit larger, some smaller, ranging in weight from 10 to 15 pounds (4.5–6.8 kg). Characteristics generally applicable to all are wedge-shaped heads and prominent eyes. They have small, rounded ears, and their hindquarters are heavily muscled, with hind legs proportionally longer than those of domestic cats.

Asian leopard cats are expert swimmers and very active climbers. In spite of their diminutive size, they are very effective, cunning, nocturnal hunters. They inhabit forests, jungles, brush country, and plains, and are usually found near water. Among their natural prey are rodents, bats, birds, fish, and occasionally young hoofed animals larger than themselves.

The estrous cycle of the wild species is much the same as that of domestic cat breeds. Predictably, the frequency of heat, mating habits, and kitten production depends upon the climate of the various Asiatic regions in which they are found. They usually have small litters, consisting of one to four kittens. In cooler climates where the females only have one estrous cycle per year, the kittens are usually born in May.

Availability of Asian Leopard Cats

Until the late 1960s, some Asian leopard cats were available in pet stores in the United States and Europe. That situation no longer exists and importation of Asian leopard cats is now prohibited or restricted, dependent upon the subspecies. Various subspecies of *F. bengalensis* are currently exhibited in the zoos of the world. Interbreeding has been reported between subspecies of *F. bengalensis* in those artificial, protected environments.

Even if specimens of *F. bengalensis* were readily available today, keeping them in your home is not advisable. Leopard cats are instinctively carnivorous hunters that may not be compatible with other house pets. When kept in captivity, they often reject, and may be threats to domestic cats. In an artificial environment, *F. bengalensis* and the first outcross generation females may kill and eat their young. A leopard cat may choose to mate with a domestic cat, but the potential difficulties do not support such a breeding endeavor by lay people.

If you are looking for a pet or companion, ownership of an Asian leopard cat is not a viable option. Wild animals do not belong in your home. Bengal cats, however, are not wild animals—they are friendly, lovable domestic house cats and no home should be without at least one!

History of the Bengal Breed

Bengals are among the newest breeds to be developed, and have only recently been added to the list of domestic cat breeds. They join the older, more populous breeds such as Siamese, Burmese, Abyssinian, Persian, and other house cats. The Bengal's history and its unique and lovely leopardlike appearance sets it clearly apart from other domestic breeds, but, like them, it was developed as a family pet. According to an estimation by The International Cat Association (TICA), its numbers have grown since 1983 to perhaps 9,000 or more registered Bengals today.

In the United States, the first intentional and controlled hybridization of a domestic cat with the wild Asian leopard cat by Jean Sugden Mill was recorded in 1965 in Arizona. Progeny from that breeding program were carried into the third generation, but none of that bloodline exists today. During the 1970s, several U.S. cat breeders again began breeding Bengal cat foundation stock and the name Bengal was adopted as the official breed name. It is believed that the bloodlines started during that period were not perpetuated.

In the early 1980s, two different Bengal bloodlines were begun by Ms. Mill. She and other Bengal enthusiasts joined forces, and through their efforts, breed standards were established and registration was undertaken by TICA. By 1984, Bengal cats from a number of bloodlines were exhibited and judged in TICA shows worldwide in the New Breed and Color class. In 1990, Bengals were accepted by TICA

Bengals love heights.

for championship competition in their shows. The Bengal is now an authentic domestic cat breed, in spite of its rather recent development. Pioneer Bengal breeder Jean Mill, who has been personally involved in all phases of the development of this fascinating breed, now resides in California where she continues to pursue her 30-year obsession with Bengals.

Exercise wheel—Jean Mill inventor, Patent Pending, Catwalk Co., Claremont, CA.

Pair of F2 youngsters.

The Bengal's Wild Ancestry

Asian leopard cats were co-progenitors of all Bengals, and their current gene pool includes a significant contribution from the wild *Felis bengalensis,* from which the Bengal's name is derived. The percentage of wild blood in a domestic Bengal is irrelevant. It may not even be possible to calculate that percentage accurately. More important is the breed standard that specifies that Bengals must have physical features distinctive to the small forest-dwelling wild cats. Special merit is given to those animals that have an appearance that sets them distinctly apart from other domestic cat breeds.

The unique genetic composition of Bengals is not all good news, however. It prevents the breed's recognition by some cat registries. It eliminates them from registration and championship competition in the shows of most cat organizations, whose rules do not allow cats with wild blood to be exhibited, irrespective of the character or disposition of the cat.

The creation and molding of the Bengal breed into its present shape has been carefully engineered by a small but increasing number of conscientious breeders. It is estimated that there are now more than 200 Bengal catteries in the United States, and many more in Canada and Europe. Interviews with professional Bengal breeders indicate that they have a common, double goal. They insist that Bengals possess predictable house-cat personalities and temperaments. Concurrently, they strive to maintain a maximum of the conformation, color, size, and coat patterns of the Asian leopard cat.

Their efforts are directed toward standardization of a breed that closely resembles the wild leopard cat, but one that can be recognized and identified as a domestic Bengal. That distinction is important from a legal and safety standpoint. For obvious reasons, veterinarians, show judges, and others who have reason to handle cats must be able to distinguish between undomesticated Asian leopard cats and docile domestic Bengal companion cats.

Ordinarily, feral cats (wild species that are not normally kept as pets) are

Three-year-old F1 female.

not registered by any cat fancy organization. TICA is a genetic registry, and therefore it allows the registration of Asian leopard cats for use only in the Bengal breeding program as foundation stock. Pedigree records are kept by TICA on all Bengals, even those that cannot compete in shows. The foundation stock of Bengals that are registered in an experimental category includes Asian leopard cats and the first three generations of outcrosses. In order to register an Asian leopard cat, TICA requires pictures and detailed information relative to the ownership, origin and location of the animal.

The reason *F. bengalensis* was used in the foundation of the Bengal breed is simple. It has strikingly beautiful colors and coat patterns. It is about the same size as the domestic cat, and it is genetically compatible with domestic cats. A major obstacle in crossing a feral cat with a domestic

is their social incompatibility. A male Asian leopard cat will usually mate with a female domestic cat, but only a limited number of successful matings between feral queens and domestic toms appear in Bengal pedigrees. The unpredictability of the attitude of a feral animal toward a domesticated animal of another species makes such breeding endeavors hazardous at best. Activities involving wild species are best left to those professionals who have the knowledge and facilities to deal with wild animals.

The Bengal's Domestic Ancestors

The Egyptian Mau is a domestic cat breed with a desirable temperament, whose spotted coat patterns breed true from generation to generation. Those and possibly other considerations made the Mau, especially the Indian variety, one of the several domestic breeds chosen to be used as domestic foundation stock that produced Bengals. Other breeds, such as the Abyssinian, Burmese, and various domestic tabby cats were used as well. In the first (F-1) generation, the coat color and patterns of Asian leopard cats tend to dominate those of domestic cats used in the outcross. In the following generations, however, the diverse genes from the domestic cats, especially those of mixed breeds, make the selection of domestic foundation breeding stock a challenge.

The breeding of wild cats to domestic cats was done to imprint the physical characteristics of a beautiful wild feline on the personality of a domestic cat. To strengthen or intensify certain conformation, coat, or color characteristics, a knowledgeable breeder may breed a domestic Bengal back to a foundation stock cat. When that is done, the progeny are considered foundation stock, and are registered in the experimental category until the fourth generation from the Asian leopard cat is attained. Only fourth generation and beyond can be considered domestic Bengals in every sense of the word.

Hybridization

The first generation Bengal cats were, by definition, hybrids. That is to say, their parents were from two different species.

The hybrid offspring of the mating of those two different species is referred to as the F-1 generation. Males of the first (F-1) generation are sterile. Therefore, in the development of Bengals, an F-1 female was bred to a domestic cat, producing the second (F-2) generation of kittens. Second generation females were bred to Bengals or other domestic cats to produce the third (F-3) generation. Sterility is observed in males of the F-2 and F-3 generations as well. Animals in those three foundation stock generations (F-1, F-2, and F-3) are not eligible for championship showing as Bengals. Together with the Asian leopard cat, they are registered by TICA in the experimental category.

Some foundation stock individuals are quite docile and may be easily handled. Others lack the desired temperament of a companion animal. Foundation stock cats are rarely kept as family pets, but in special cases, they may be placed in carefully selected homes that meet certain criteria and restrictions.

Bengals of the F-4 generation and beyond are uniformly acceptable as family pets. The breeders of Bengals select their propagation stock according to each animal's conformity to breed standards, including disposition and physical characteristics, irrespective of their percentage of wild blood.

There is some minimal risk involved in keeping any pet in a human household, but most domestic companion animals, both dogs and cats, pose little threat to their human housemates except when they are injured or abused.

Understanding Bengal Cats

Bengals are delightfully safe pets to own. They easily meet the breed standards that require loving, dependable temperaments, although individuals of any breed may be less desirable than others. The potential for their reversion to the disposition of their feral ancestors is remote.

The disposition of Bengals is comparable to that of many other domestic cat breeds. Typically, they are outgoing, curious, playful, and affectionate pets. They are rarely timid or reclusive and they easily blend into the social order of their family and bond to its members. Bengals enjoy gentle handling and grooming by adults and children alike. They are happy, responsive souls that possess exceptional intelligence and trainability.

Comments frequently heard from Bengal owners dwell on their inherent mental keenness. Some believe that the breed has a skull size that is proportionally larger than other domestic breeds, and suggest that may be associated with greater brain mass and capacity. Bengals are not vocal cats that pester their owners, wanting to give their opinions on every subject, but they will converse when given the opportunity and when encouraged to do so. An interesting short, rather guttural barking sound is sometimes heard from Bengals, especially when fed some particularly tasty treat.

The Aquatic Bengal

Bengals are reputed to have an affinity for water. Many will take an uninvited dip in the bathtub with their owners, and others have a propensity to share the shower or lavatory with their human companions. Bengal kittens frequently play in their water bowls, and their toys are often found floating about in their dishes.

My grandson's Bengal kitten, Simba, delights in playing with tub toys in a large plastic bowl or dishpan half full of water. Simba wades up to his belly, puts his head under water to

Your Bengal may join you in the tub.

The Climbing Bengal

Another Bengal peculiarity is its affinity for height. Breeding kennels are usually fitted out with platforms near the ceiling, where the resident Bengal is frequently found in regal posture, surveying its estate. Bengals are accomplished climbers, and spend a good deal of time in trees or on high climbing posts when available. Bengals are very surefooted creatures with extraordinary athletic abilities that would be expected in cats with their heritage. They are busy pets that enjoy exercise, and most will use large running wheels similar to the small ones found in hamster cages. Their sleek, trim, athletic conformation and solid musculature is enhanced by their instinctive climbing and running exercises.

Bengals are very positive, independent animals, not at all shy or withdrawn. They freely accept other animals, but they are not likely to be found at the bottom of the pecking order of the household pets. They commonly share their space on an equal basis with other breeds of cats

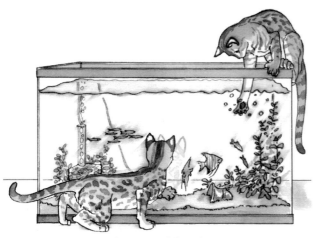

Cover your fish tank.

retrieve toys, then snorts the water from his nose and dives in again. No data is available relative to Bengals' habits around household fish tanks, but it may be wise to cover your tanks if they are within reach of an adventuresome Bengal.

Climbing to a cozy shelf on the play tree.

16

This Bengal displays excellent marble pattern on appropriately long body.

and with dogs. They are not fragile or timid, neither are they contrary nor aggressive. Handling a Bengal is like handling any other cat. If treated gently when young, a kitten will grow up to be a gentle cat. If a cat of any breed is treated roughly, abused, or frightened consistently, it will become reclusive, defensive, and resentful.

Children should be carefully instructed in the proper handling of kittens or any other small pets. Generally, tiny tots and tiny kittens should be watched closely when together. There is more danger of a child injuring a Bengal kitten than the opposite.

Appearance

A handsome Bengal's coat should be soft and smooth like a pelt. There are two coat patterns recognized, spotted and marbled.

The popular spotted pattern closely resembles the Asian leopard cat's appearance. Spotted Bengals have dark spots on a contrasting lighter background color. The spots take vari-

ous shapes and are arranged in a horizontal alignment over the body, or sometimes in a random configuration. That differs from the vertical spotting patterns and stripes found on tabbies and other breeds. Rosette spots, common to the wild leopard cats, have multishaded light centers or shadows on the dark spots. Rosettes are quite striking in appearance, and are very desirable. Bengals are the only domestic purebreds that possess rosettes, and the genetics of their transmission is still being worked out by Bengal breeders.

The marbled pattern is uniquely different from the spotted pattern, and it also has great eye appeal. Although wild felines such as the clouded leopard demonstrate marbling, Asian leopard cats in the Bengal ancestry are not known to possess that coat pattern. Marbled Bengals are believed to result from domestic butterfly tabbies that were used in early development of Bengals. The multishade, horizontally aligned rosettes of Asian leopard cats

17

somehow influence the marbling characteristic, resulting in the Bengal's horizontally flowing marble patterns.

Marbled Bengals' dark whorls on a lighter background should have several distinctive outlines of slightly darker colors. An article by Jean Mill, ("Marble influence on Bengal spots," *TIBCS Newsletter*) explains that the outlining seems to be more prominent if the Asian leopard cat in the family tree was markedly rosetted. The breeder tells of a Bengal male that is both spotted and marbled.

The desired marble pattern has a random horizontal flow on the side of the cat that is distinctly different from the bull's-eye patterns in butterfly tabby cats. Vertical stripes, commonly seen in mackerel tabbies, are undesirable in Bengals. Bengal color and pattern genetics are complex. The relationship of marbled to spotted patterns in Bengals is the subject of intense investigation.

There are presently three Bengal colors recognized: the brown tabby, the seal lynx point, and the seal sepia tabby/seal mink tabby. All Bengals should have black or nearly black tips on their tails, and light-colored, spotted bellies. Bengals weigh up to about 15 pounds (6.8 kg) and have small, rounded ears and a slightly Roman nose. Many Bengals have prominent white tactile whisker pads on their muzzles that are very distinctive. Bengals have trim, well-knit, powerful bodies, similar to those of Asian leopard cats.

Pets Versus Show Cats

A Bengal is a Bengal is a Bengal. Right? Wrong! A pet-quality Bengal differs from a show-quality cat, which differs from a breeding-quality animal. All three may meet the minimum standards for the breed, but purchase prices will vary greatly. There should, however, be no difference between the personalities of the various qualities of Bengals. A fancy show-winning Bengal's disposition should be just as desirable as that of a pet-quality cat, and vice versa.

Breeders who are now propagating the many different Bengal bloodlines are naturally developing minute differences in the appearance of their cats that tend to identify their own lines. They study the individuals that possess the various desirable characteristics, and through careful selection of breeding stock, they strengthen and fix those features in their bloodlines.

The acceptable variations in physical conformation, coat, and color, may be more or less desirable, depending on the purpose for which the cat is acquired. Before purchasing a Bengal for showing or breeding purposes, the breed standard should be memorized. At the same time, winning Bengals in the show rings should be studied to establish a personal knowledge of the best of the breed.

If acquisition of a pet Bengal is the goal, selection should be made according to the appeal of an animal to the buyer. Consideration should always be given to the breed standard and the conformity of the cat to that standard, but the eye appeal, personality, and health of a pet are equally important. Show-quality faults may be easily overlooked by a pet buyer if a kitten is particularly winsome, affectionate, active, and healthy. Pet cats should be castrated or spayed at or before maturity, and many pet-quality kittens are sold without registration papers. You may want your Bengal to look like other Bengals, but rigid compliance with all the standards applied to show cats does not increase the companion value of a pet Bengal.

Rosettes.

Bengal Ownership

A Bengal cat requires about the same care as cats of other breeds. It is not encumbered with a finicky appetite or objectionable habits. It is easily litter box trained and can be kept in your home all its life with little special attention. There are, however, many factors to consider before you decide upon the addition of a Bengal or any other cat to your household. First, you must love cats.

Cat lovers are found in all walks of life, and in every conceivable circumstance. They are the fortunate individuals who have come to appreciate cats as housemates. Many people are hooked into ownership of a cat under false pretenses. They hear about the independence and undemanding character of cats as pets, and they believe it! A few weeks later their homes are arrayed with a dozen pieces of cat furniture, and their pantry shelves are stocked with a variety of cat foods and treats. Their lives are wonderfully enriched by the presence of a royal dignitary with a name like Sweetcakes. They clean litter boxes, sleep with furry tails in their faces, and awake to the tune of loud feline motors—all for the honor of sharing their lives with 10 pounds (4.5 kg) of fur and purr.

They resent any suggestion that they have some deep attachment to their cats, and they swear that when Sweetcakes is gone, they will never have another pet. Deep inside, however, the thought of being without a cat in the family is untenable. Within the ranks of cat lovers are those who are attached to specific breeds of cats.

They have discovered that individuals of certain breeds are more interesting and have more charisma and charm than others.

Why Own a Bengal?

Certain personality characteristics are passed from generation to generation in all breeds. Some breeds, such as the Siamese, have the reputation (earned or not) of being more vocal than others. The dignified Persians are sometimes thought of as laid-back cats who seem always to be on display in a store window. What can be said about the Bengal?

Bengal cats combine many of the majestic physical features of Asian leopard cats with the lovable personalities of domestic house cats. Their appearance is startling at first, and will be the topic of conversations with

Variety of cat furnishings.

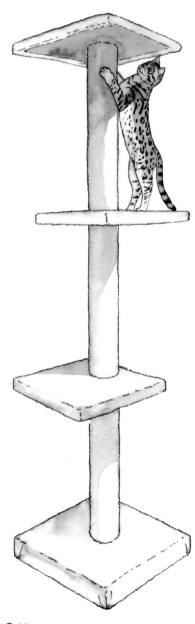

Cat tower.

your friends. Sometimes guests are taken off guard when an adult Bengal strolls regally into a room, but the immediate shock reaction is quickly replaced by admiration.

If you are fascinated by rare and unique personalities, you will undoubtedly enjoy the companionship of a Bengal. If you appreciate the unusual, a Bengal pet may be an excellent choice for you. Don't be surprised the first time your Bengal joins you in the bathtub, or when you first discover it lying in royal posture, surveying its kingdom from some almost inaccessibly high vantage point.

Bengals typically are not aggressive pets, but if you expect to find an inanimate couch potato clad in the beautiful colors and patterns of a Bengal, you will be disappointed. As in other breeds, each animal is endowed with its own personality, but Bengals characteristically are genial, active, amusing, and companionable pets with an essence of the jungle.

Cost of a Bengal

There is no such thing as a free pet. Even a kitten that is taken in as a refugee from a storm, or is found on your doorstep, has costs associated with its care. The Bengal kitten that you choose to share your home and life will be your companion for a very long time. Cats often live to ripe old ages, many as long as 15 or 18 years. The initial cost of purchase reflects the magnitude of your desire to have a particular Bengal cat. However, the financial obligations associated with the day by day ownership of a Bengal are no greater than those associated with ownership of a free tabby. Costs are offset by hundreds of joyful hours that a feline companion will bring to your life. Cat lovers receive daily rewards for the time and money they invest in their pets.

You can expect to pay for the rarity of a Bengal. Because of the newness of the breed and the time, difficulty, and cost of producing such unique creatures, Bengals command a rather high price. The purchase cost depends upon many factors. If you are shopping for an animal with very few breed faults and one that will hold its own in championship showing, you are probably looking at a price of $1,000 to $3,000 or more. Prices in the same range or slightly higher, are charged for breeding stock, because only the best animals are used to perpetuate the breed, and many breeding-quality animals have cat show titles.

Pet Bengals are a bit easier on the purse. Depending upon the quality of the individual, Bengal kittens that are sold as pets range in price from $200 to $500. Some may be sold for less if they have significant undesirable flaws in their conformation, color, or coat patterns. On occasion, some pet Bengal kittens are even given away to good homes by a breeder. You should expect strict requirements attached to a pet kitten. Some breeders will only part with them if the new owner guarantees that the pet will be confined to your home and altered at maturity.

Confinement for kitten or queen in season.

The costs of food and veterinary service for a Bengal are no different from those incurred for any other cat. If you are planning to cut the costs of ownership by buying the cheapest brand of food for your Bengal, or ignoring its health care, you may be disappointed in the results. The costs of food and litter are nominal. Like health care, those ongoing costs are a necessary part of pet ownership.

Getting Ready for Your Bengal Kitten

The first consideration when deciding to buy a Bengal is your ability and desire to take care of the new pet. Are you willing and able to provide for it for the next ten or 15 years? That is a question sometimes ignored by prospective pet owners. In the United States, thousands of cats in shelters and pounds are destroyed daily for want of suitable homes. The purchase of a beautiful new Bengal kitten is an event to celebrate, but be sure that you understand the obligation you are taking upon yourself.

For its safety, your Bengal should be confined to your home day and night. To do otherwise is to contribute to the already overwhelming problem of stray and abandoned cats. Cats that are allowed out of the house, even briefly, often meet with disaster.

Cat Furniture

Certain items are needed by your new companion. Its bed need be nothing more than a small cardboard box with an old towel or sweater for bedding. Instead, it might be an expensive, multiroom cat condo, replete with one or more cozy, carpeted little snoozing rooms, stairs, perches, and platforms. Bengals love heights, so if you purchase a cat condominium, choose one with a high observation platform. Commercially manufactured cat furniture is expensive but very durable.

A litter box is another essential. Any impermeable, flat-bottomed container will work. It should have sides at least 4 or 6 inches (10–15.2 cm) tall to contain the litter. Manufactured litter boxes are available in pet supply stores. Some come equipped with covers, swinging doors, and deodorant dispensers.

Commercial litter is made of small clay particles that are very absorptive, facilitating the litter box cleaning process. Litter cost depends on the packaging, the deodorants used, and the brand names. To find the one that works best for you, experiment with different litter products, using a small bag of one, then another. Some litter material has a propensity to stick to the hair of a cat's feet and fall onto the carpet. Others have perfumes that are objectionable to cats. Some products cause urine to clump, making cleaning easier. (If ingested, clumping litter can cause severe problems in kittens, and its use is not recommended for them.) Litter pan liners are plastic bags that can be used inside a litter pan to facilitate dumping the litter and excrement easily, with less mess.

Hiding Places

A place of refuge is another must, especially if there are children or other pets in the family. Every cat, no matter what its age, needs a place to go when it wants to be left alone for a nap. When a kitten is frightened by the noise of children, or is being harassed by the family poodle, or when it tires of playing, it will seek out its hiding place. A cardboard box about 12 or 14 inches (30.5–35.6 cm) square, with a top on it, works fine for that purpose.

Bengal sharpening claws on an overturned carpet swatch.

Cut a hole in one end, just large enough to allow the kitten to enter. Put an old towel or some article of your clothing in the box, and place it in a secluded place.

The top platform of a cat condo is a favorite refuge for adult Bengals. Sometimes kittens will choose their own hiding spot, such as behind a sofa or under the bed or another piece of furniture. Any cozy location that is inaccessible to other pets is acceptable. It is important that all members of the family honor your Bengal's place of refuge.

Scratching Posts

The outer layers of cats' retractable claws flake off normally. All cats extend their claws and scratch on something to facilitate that normal flaking. Soft bark of young trees is one of the preferred natural materials for working their nails. Because most homes don't have trees growing in them, your indoor Bengal will probably use a chair or sofa. Due to the cost of

reupholstering furniture, that habit is rarely acceptable, so it is best to have a scratching post in place when you bring the kitten home. You can make such a post out of a short section of soft wood, or you can buy a fancy commercial model, covered with carpet or sisal rope. Although the manufactured models cost more than a piece of wood nailed to a platform, they last for years.

Some cats prefer to work their claws on carpet. In that case, provide a swatch of discarded carpet material about 18 inches (45.7 cm) square. Lay the carpet swatch on the floor upside down, so your Bengal can work its claws into the jute backing.

Another innovative scratching product has recently been introduced in the cat furniture market. It consists of a small, paddle-shaped piece of wood, wound tightly with sisal rope. It can be laid on the floor or hung from a doorknob by an attached rope loop.

Grooming Tools

A brush and a fine comb, manufactured specifically for cats, should be

Healthy kittens at play.

Morning playtime: an F2 and an F3 kitten.

water is kept in them continuously. Some plastics may also release chemicals into the water after it has been kept in the dish for a long period of time.

The Security of Confinement

A culture shock must be expected when a kitten is taken from its mother, the security of its nursery, and the companionship of its littermates. The trauma of changing environments can be minimized by confinement of the newcomer for a few days when it arrives in your home. That is especially important if there are children or other pets in the house, or if the adults are gone from the house during the day. Confinement in a bathroom works well, but any small room that you can temporarily rig as a halfway house will do. The less furniture in the room, the better. If it is impossible to appropriate a small confinement room for a week or so, consider the purchase of a large wire kennel from a pet supply store.

Boarding Your Pet

If you plan to be gone from home occasionally, you should plan in advance for your Bengal's care during your absence. A clean, well-recommended cat boarding facility may be chosen, but better yet is a friend who will stop in at your home every day to check on your cat. Cats are happier and at less risk of accident or illness in their own homes. If someone can be found who will clean the litter box regularly and provide fresh water and food daily, that is ideal. Another possibility to consider is a friend who will take the Bengal into her or his home and provide for it there.

Medical Services

Health care is of extreme importance. Bengals are notoriously hardy cats, but accidents happen, even in the most careful families. If you do not already have a professional relation-

purchased. If fleas are indigenous to your area, a very fine-tooth flea comb will help to identify those parasites on your Bengal.

Nail trimmers of various designs are available, but, the best ones are those that cut the nail cleanly with no crushing effect that causes pain to your pet. Because nails should be trimmed every couple of weeks, be sure that you make the procedure as quick and painless as possible.

Food and Water Dishes

The safest vessels to use are stainless steel food and water dishes that are available in pet supply stores. Some ceramic dishes have been reported to release paint or firing chemicals when

Cuddling up with Mom for a quick afternoon nap.

ship with a local veterinarian, establish one before bringing your kitten home. You can sometimes find one who has special expertise or training in cat health, but most companion animal clinicians have adequate interest and knowledge of feline medicine and surgery. There are a number of subjects that should be discussed with your veterinarian.

• a preventive health care plan for the kitten, including vaccination and physical examination schedules

• the possibility of health insurance

• subscription to a pet health newsletter

• dietary advice, including vitamin supplementation

• the availability of emergency care

If possible, make an appointment to meet the veterinarian and discuss those topics before you acquire your kitten. Then take the kitten to the veterinarian before you take it home. A brief physical examination may reveal some obscure problem. If such a problem is discovered immediately, and you don't want to deal with it, the breeder will likely agree to replace the kitten. Although that thought may be very distasteful to you, it is far better to deal with problems as soon as they are discovered, before the inevitable attachment has joined you and your Bengal.

Shopping for Your Purebred Bengal

There are estimated to be over 200 Bengal catteries in the United States. The Bengal breed is rapidly becoming more popular in Canada and Europe where hundreds more Bengal breeders may be found. U.S. Bengal breed clubs publish bimonthly newsletters, and cat magazines often print Bengal advertisements (See Useful Addresses and Literature, page 91). These listings will help you find a Bengal of your liking without traveling too far.

Be very cautious when you purchase a Bengal. Not all spotted cats are Bengals. There are many counterfeits floating around, some with authentic looking pedigrees. Unscrupulous people have been known to purchase a Bengal of pet quality, breed it to a backyard tabby, and advertise the offspring as purebred Bengals. That kind of unethical activity often accompanies the development of a new breed when public knowledge is sketchy and when prices are high.

When you shop for a Bengal from any source, you should first study the breed standards carefully. If possible, visit at least one Bengal cattery and look at their breeding stock as well as the kittens available. Look at the parents and siblings of a kitten before you buy it. Compare those animals with the breed standards and with other Bengal cats in the cattery and ask about perceived differences.

An informed, legitimate Bengal source will have the answers, and will discuss them with you. If the seller is unable or unwilling to show you the kittens' parents or some of the kitten's family, and he or she is not well prepared to answer your questions about the kitten, run, don't walk, to the nearest exit.

Cat Shows

Try to attend a cat show where you can personally watch the top Bengals of the country in competition for ribbons and titles. See what a Grand Champion Bengal looks like, face to face. Visualize, in living color, the various patterns and markings of the breed. If it is your intention to purchase a Bengal to show or breed, it is imperative that you attend at least one or two shows before you choose your kitten.

When you attend a cat show, pick up business cards from breeders who have kittens for sale. Bengal breeders who show their cats are the best people to help you begin your kitten search. Information about shows may be obtained from cat associations and clubs and from cat magazines (See Useful Addresses and Literature, page 91).

If you cannot attend a cat show, the breeders of Bengals in your area are easily located through ads they place in the various Bengal newsletters and in cat magazines.

Newsletters

The next best source of Bengal breeder information is a breed club newsletter (see Bengal Breed Clubs, page 92). Editors of newsletters may send you a free copy. If not, subscription prices are reasonable.

Newspapers

Other sources of Bengal kittens are found in classified ads in newspapers, wherein many ethical breeders advertise their Bengal kittens. Unfortunately, a few disreputable opportunists also advertise in newspapers. That comment is not meant to discourage the potential Bengal owner from contacting breeders who advertise in the paper, only to inspire the prospective buyer's awareness. Ask lots of questions, examine the seller's Bengal knowledge, and look closely at their facilities as well as their kittens and breeding stock.

Kitten Mills

Kitten mills are places (often private homes) that house a collection of registered, purebred cats of both sexes and often of several different breeds.

Kitten mill management gives little attention to the breed standards of their animals. Their goal is making money from the sale of mass-produced kittens. Few exhibit their breeding stock in cat shows. The value of cats in a kitten mill lies in their ability to reproduce, not in their conformation or personalities. Kittens thus produced are often marketed through newspaper ads and sometimes through pet shops. The health and quality of Bengals originating in kitten factories are always suspect. It is best to avoid kitten mills as a source of your Bengal.

Mixed Bengals

Be especially wary of ads that offer mixed Bengal kittens, or Bengals without pedigree or registration. When the kittens offered are the progeny of the mating of a purebred to a mixed breed, the genetic makeup of the kittens is complex. Another kitten may be from the mating of two mixed breeds, and so on.

If you should happen to find a healthy spotted kitten that is purported to be a mixed Bengal, and if its appearance and personality strike your fancy, buy it. There is absolutely nothing wrong with a mixed Bengal if it is obtained for the correct reasons. It carries the genes of different personalities, colors, and sizes of cats. Its value is exactly the same as any other backyard bred cat, and its cost should be the same as that of an average tabby or calico.

The Age of Your New Kitten

Every year thousands of kittens of all breeds and mixtures are weaned and sold or given away when they are five, six, or seven weeks old. Kittens may eat solid food as early as three or four weeks of age, although they are rarely weaned by their dam before six to eight weeks. I have personally known great numbers of kittens that

Author's grandson's kitten in bowl of water.

were snatched away from their mothers and siblings at or before six weeks of age. Some adapted to the environmental changes admirably, and lived happy, healthy, well-adjusted lives.

Many kittens that are taken from their nursery environment too soon suffer from that early separation and carry personality scars for the rest of their lives. I have known many that nursed on blankets, other animals' tails, or human fingers. Others are difficult to litter train, and some become vocal nuisances.

To avoid those problems, many cat breeders employ a safety first policy—keeping all kittens until a certain age, usually three months.

Many Bengal breeders do not release kittens until they have received one or two vaccinations. To observe the development of their conformation, colors, and coat patterns, some breeders keep their kittens until they are several months old.

I do not advocate taking kittens from their siblings and dams at an early age. Neither do I find fault with placing a particularly independent and adventuresome, strong, healthy kitten into a carefully selected new home before the traditional 12 weeks of age. The determining factor is its maturity, not its age. Some kittens are not ready to leave the nursery at 12 weeks. Kittens are individuals, and the time for each to leave the nest is best judged by the breeder, who has the opportunity to watch the litter from birth.

If a very young kitten is acquired, special consideration must be given to its diet, safety, and health. That special care should be discussed both with the breeder and with your veterinarian.

Try a Mature Pet

Purchase of an older Bengal must also be considered. Sometimes cats become available after they have passed the kitten stage. Acquiring an

Goin' fishin'.

older, but still youthful, pet denies you the fun and experiences related to the frisky two- or three-month-old kitten. At the same time, you will be compensated in several ways for that loss. The initial vaccination costs have already been absorbed. The time of greatest susceptibility to infectious diseases has passed. A cat acquired at six months or one year of age will likely be more stable. Barring some disaster, your Bengal will probably live at least 12 years, very likely longer. If it has received the proper attention and handling during its kittenhood, an older kitten or young adult might be a real bargain.

Choosing the Sex

As you begin to look at available kittens, you should consider the sex of the Bengal in your future. If your intention is to breed Bengals, obviously a female is the right choice. At the outset, you must accept the fact that there is precious little monetary reward realized by most cat breeders. Their motives are, or should be, improvement of the breed through the production of the highest possible quality kittens from the best breeding stock available. Making a significant profit is a dubious goal at best.

To produce show- and breeding-quality kittens, you must begin with a breeding-quality female. You must contend with a queen that comes in season every few weeks when she is not pregnant. Cat show expenses may be burdensome. A cat breeder must be able and ready to interview prospective buyers, and to search for acceptable homes for all of the kittens in each litter.

When you shop for a breeding queen, you will find that those available are expensive and somewhat limited in number. If a pet is desired, and you are not planning to breed your Bengal, either sex will do, the number of kittens available for your selection will be dramatically increased, and prices will reflect the increased supply.

Females

Before choosing a pet Bengal, you should know something about the sexual activities of cats, so that you can make a more informed decision about which gender you prefer. Female cats have an estrus cycle of 20 to 30 days that begins at about six or seven months of age. The period of visible estrous, also known as being "in heat" or "in season," happens once every three to four weeks, and females stay in season for five to 14 days. Many indoor queens' estrous cycles continue to repeat year-round. The outward signs of a queen in heat are usually very apparent, sometimes even bizarre.

Females in season exhibit many peculiar and erratic signs, and a resolute desire to escape from the house. They rub their chins, necks, and faces on the carpet while holding their hindquarters elevated and their tails off to one side. Queens in heat may be uncommonly affectionate toward

Posture of queen in season.

humans or other pet companions. They yowl and cry in strange voices, sometimes in the middle of the night. They often roll about on the floor with their bodies gyrating. When petted, they elevate their rear quarters in an exaggerated manner with each hand stroke along the back. Their appetites are often decreased.

Male cats of the neighborhood are attracted to your home when your queen is in season. They hear her mournful crying and set up camp outside the window, as eager to meet the queen as she is to find a mate. Sometimes more than one tom is attracted to the queen's home and the din of brawling tom cats fills the night.

If she happens to escape from her confinement and slips out of the house for a few minutes, she will probably return in a family way. If that happens, you must assume the responsibilities that accompany her pregnancy, raising and finding homes for her brood of mixed kittens. If you do not wish to face those prospects, there is a better way to care for your female Bengal pet.

Spaying (ovariohysterectomy): Spaying a young, healthy queen is a surgical procedure that is performed dozens of times a week in busy veteri-

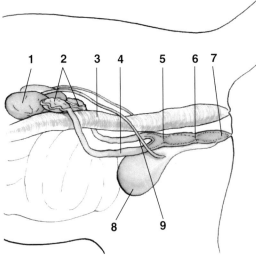

Female genitalia. 1 = Left Kidney, 2 = Ovaries, 3 = Colon, 4 = Left uterine horn, 5 = Uterine body, 6 = Cervix, 7 = Vagina, 8 = Urinary bladder, 9 = Left ureter.

nary practices. Major, irreversible, abdominal surgery should not be taken lightly, but because it is an operation that is done so frequently, the techniques used are well developed and are very safe in the hands of an experienced veterinary surgeon. An abdominal incision is made just behind the navel, and both ovaries and the uterus are removed. The patient is often allowed to return home the same day or early the next day, as soon as she has fully recovered from the anesthetic. Complications from the operation are rare, aftercare is minimal, and your Bengal should be eating and playing normally within a few days.

The advantages to spaying your queen are many. The cat's estrous cycle no longer occurs, her personality and habits are more predictable, and she will concentrate more on her human companions. Registered spayed females can be shown in alter classes in cat shows.

The fee for spaying a queen varies so much from one area of the country to another that it is impossible to provide meaningful fee estimates. Take your pet to your veterinarian and ask him or her to quote a fee for the surgery and to explain the plan for having it done. The ideal time to spay your cat is at about six months of age, before she comes into heat the first time. She can be spayed while she is showing the signs of estrus, and even if she has been bred, spaying is a viable option if done in a timely manner. Talk to your Bengal's doctor about scheduling such surgery.

Males

If you decide upon a male Bengal pet, you can expect him to reach puberty at about six to ten months of age. Like queens, males also have a heat cycle. It begins at puberty and is continuous from that day forward until they die or are castrated. At puberty,

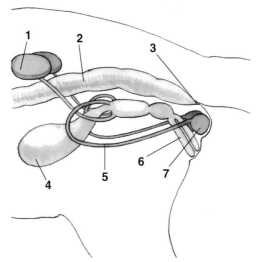

Male genitalia. 1 = Left kidney, 2 = Colon, 3 = Anus, 4 = Urinary bladder, 5 = Left vas deferens, 6 = Retracted penis, 7 = Left testicle.

males begin to show evidence of wanting to hit the streets to pursue their reproductive instincts. They become more aggressive toward other male cats, and if other unneutered males (toms) are in the household, skirmishes will probably occur. They may remain affectionate and docile toward their human companions, females, and altered cats, but sexually mature toms are difficult to keep in a home environment.

Male cats make their presence known by spraying very foul-smelling urine on vertical surfaces, such as doors, drapes, or furniture. It is an instinctive territory marking technique peculiar to all domestic and wild cats. The terribly offensive urine of adult males is sprayed to invite queens into their territories and to warn other toms that they are in residence and will defend their bailiwicks against intruders.

If an outdoor queen in season senses the tom's presence, she will camp under your window, yowling,

A Bengal mother teaching proper hunting technique to her attentive kitten.

inviting him to visit with her. He may become aggressive in his attempt to comply with her amatory invitation. If not allowed outside, he will likely spray his scent promiscuously about the house.

If he escapes from the house, he may return bloodied, and in need of medical care from encounters with other neighborhood males. You must also accept responsibility for his significant contribution to the unwanted kitten population of the neighborhood. After all, a queen can only produce a couple of litters a year, but a tom can breed all available queens every night. For those reasons, most people prefer to have their adult, unneutered male pets castrated at about the time puberty is reached.

Castration (Orchiectomy):
Castrating (neutering) a male cat usually costs less than half the fee charged for spaying a female. It is a simpler procedure with fewer potential complications, and shorter anesthesia

time is required. The operation includes surgical removal of both testicles, usually through an incision in the scrotum. Typically, the cat is sent home the same day of the surgery. Young cats begin to eat and play the following day. The ideal time to castrate a male is at about eight or nine months of age. However, if he begins to show signs of wanderlust or spraying before that age, your pet can be neutered earlier. Castration is not the same as a vasectomy, and as in a spay operation, the surgery is not reversible.

The advantages of castration are many. Attitude changes may be dramatic. Neutered males are more human oriented and predictable. They lose the desire to escape from the house at every opportunity, and if they get outside, they are less likely to get into trouble. The propensity to spray urine ceases and their urine loses its rank odor. Neutered males may also be shown in classes for altered cats.

Cathays Simba *and author's grandson, Tyler.*

Choosing a Healthy Kitten

After you have decided the future for your Bengal, you can begin the process of selecting your pet. A great deal can be learned about the health and personality of kittens by watching a group at play. You should look for a kitten that appears bright, mischievous, and alert. Choose one that is adventuresome and friendly. Select a kitten that comes to you if possible. One that hides and remains quiet is probably not ready to leave the nest.

Kittens that sit with their heads down, disinterested in their surroundings, are probably not well. If quiet, lethargic kittens are seen in a group, ask the breeder about them. If kittens sneeze or have discharge from their noses or eyes, go home and return in another week—or choose another source for your Bengal. Do not purchase a kitten that appears unwell, no matter what guarantee is offered.

Drag a toy in front of the kittens and watch their response. Healthy, alert kittens show immediate curiosity and playfulness. When you pick a kitten up and hold it close to your body, it should feel soft and squirmy with a clean, soft coat.

Look at its eyes. They should be bright and clear, without redness or discharge. The color of the nose pad depends somewhat upon the bloodline of the Bengal, but it should always be damp and clean, without any caking or discharge from the nostrils. A healthy kitten's skin is supple and when a small section of skin over the back of the neck is gently lifted and released, it should immediately snap back. If it doesn't, the kitten may be dehydrated, an indication of disease. The membranes in its mouth should be bright pink.

Registration of Your Bengal Kitten

With your purebred Bengal, you should receive several important documents including a pedigree and registration.

Pedigree

A pedigree is not a registration document. It is a genealogical chart of your pet's ancestors, showing their names and show titles. It gains importance if you decide to show or breed your Bengal, otherwise it is only a coat of arms. It will list an Asian leopard cat if your kitten is in the fourth generation from that ancestor. In other words, the pedigree customarily lists the parents, grandparents, and great-grandparents of your kitten. Some breeders keep extensive pedigrees of all kittens that they produce, and can furnish as much background information as desired. For a fee, The International Cat Association (TICA) will furnish either three- or five-gener-

Several documents should accompany the kitten.

ation pedigrees to owners of cats that are registered by that association.

Registering Your Bengal

Registration papers will originate from whichever association registered the parents. Most Bengals being produced today are registered with TICA. Some are registered with the Cat Fanciers Federation (CFF), and a few with the American Cat Fanciers Association (ACFA). (See Cat Associations, page 91.)

When the breeder registers a litter with TICA, an *Application for Registration of a Cat of a Registered Litter* (blue slip) is furnished to the breeder for each kitten in the litter. The blue slip that you receive lists the kitten's birth date, color, sex, and eye color. You choose a name for the kitten and put it and information about yourself on the blue slip, and then you mail it to TICA with a registration fee. The permanent registration certificate is sent to you within a few weeks. At the present time, TICA's fee for permanent registration of a litter-registered kitten is $7.

If you purchase a cat that has already been permanently registered, you will receive the permanent registration document that includes the official name of the cat. You and the former owner must then initiate a transfer of ownership on the reverse of the registration document. That form is then mailed to TICA where the signatures are verified and the changes in registration are affected. The owner's name is changed on the registration documents by TICA. The registration number and name of the cat stay the same, but the new owner may add their TICA-registered cattery name as a suffix. The fee for transfer of registration is also currently $7.

If you purchase a pet-quality kitten, you may be asked to co-sign a document (contract) that specifies that the cat will be spayed or neutered at your expense, by a certain age. Registration papers on pet kittens are sometimes withheld by the breeder until the cat has been spayed or neutered. There are no universal rules governing this practice, and the legality or ethics of the practice are debated frequently among breeders and buyers. Reach a clear understanding on that subject with the breeder before ownership changes hands.

Show or Breeding Agreement

If you purchase a Bengal that is represented by the breeder to be of show quality, that should be stated in a separate signed document. Such a document should also define a show-quality cat, and state what recourse you have if the Bengal does not perform to the level of the breeder's expectation. Technically, any registered Bengal of the fourth generation or beyond may be entered in a show, but few will place or win in their classes.

If Bengals are sold as breeding stock, their progeny is another measure of their quality. If the breeder of your kitten feels strongly that it can produce offspring that possess equal or better qualities than it displays, there should be some agreement in writing specifying how the breeder will back up those claims. Such an agreement may identify the mates to use to attain the quality of kittens desired. If

you pay a premium for a breeding or show animal, something more than registration and pedigree papers are due you.

Health and Vaccination Record

A document should be furnished that lists the names and dates for all vaccinations given, as well as the person's name who administered the vaccinations. It should cite the recommended date for booster vaccinations as well.

If your kitten was seen by a veterinarian for any reason, the date and purpose of the visits should be shown, as well as the name and address of the veterinarian consulted. Results of fecal examinations and worm treatments, including the dates and name of the products used, should be listed. The health and vaccination record, or a copy of it, should be given to your veterinarian.

Dietary Information

You should receive a record of your kitten's diet, including the type of food (canned, semimoist, or dry), brand name, and quantity of each kind of food that is being fed. You may change its food, but all changes in diet should be made gradually. It is therefore important to know exactly what is being fed when you take it home. If the kitten is receiving any supplements such as cottage cheese, meat, eggs, vitamins, or minerals, they should also be listed, together with the quantity being fed.

Male displaying spotted belly.

Twelve-week-old F2 female.

F2 male.

Bringing Your Bengal Kitten Home

Transporting Your Kitten

If you purchase your Bengal out of town, transportation is easy. Cats travel well and safely in enclosed carriers, especially in fiberglass air travel models, with ventilation holes on all sides and a steel mesh safety door on the front. You can expect to hear some complaints from the caged kitty for the first few miles on the road, but it will usually quiet down after it becomes accustomed to the motion of the vehicle.

The kitten will travel better if you place in the carrier some familiar article of bedding. Tranquilization of a cat for the purpose of traveling is rarely necessary or advisable.

If your new Bengal is to travel by air, it will do well in the same type of

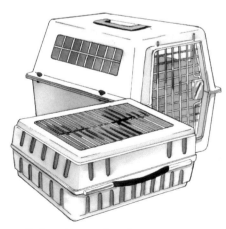

Preferred types of carriers.

fiberglass carrier. A cat in its carrier travels in a pressurized and temperature-controlled compartment on the plane. If you decide to take the cat with you into the passenger compartment, be sure to check in advance with the airline regarding the size of carrier that is allowed. Cats are not usually allowed to travel on any public transportation unless they are confined to a carrier.

When to Bring Your Kitten Home

To begin your exciting new role as a Bengal owner, you should choose the best possible time to bring the new pet into your home. Young Bengals are loving creatures that will absorb as much attention as you can provide. The more time you give to the kitten, the quicker it will bond and adjust to its new home and family.

A poor time to bring a new pet home is when the household routine is about to be disrupted, such as during busy holiday seasons. The confusion of new faces, voices, and hands may overwhelm the kitten and deter from its adjustment to a new environment. Each family has its best and worst times to introduce a new member into its midst. Try to choose a time when stability reigns.

If you want an adult pet that is gentle, fun, and affectionate, treat your kitten with gentleness, play with it, and give it as much loving attention as time will allow during those first weeks. It will be a kitten only a few months, but it will be an adult for more than ten years. The rules that you promulgate and the habits that you promote early will last for its lifetime.

Similarly, if anyone treats the kitten roughly, teases or frightens it during that formative period, you may harvest the sour fruits of those seeds for the next ten or 15 years.

Even if your Bengal is several months old when obtained, its personality traits are not set in concrete. The most pliant period of its life may have passed, but its habits are still subject to change. The treatment it receives will affect its habits and temperament for life.

Training Your Kitten

By the time a Bengal kitten is old enough to leave its nursery, it will very likely be perfectly litter box trained. However, young kittens tend to play so hard that they may not have time to search out a litter box. Training can be reinforced by confinement for a few days in a small room with a litter box handy.

Train your kitten to accept regular grooming as soon as the kitten arrives in your home. Use a soft cat brush and a fine-tooth cat comb. A few minutes of gentle combing and brushing should be repeated at least daily for the first few weeks. Kittens appreciate the quality time spent in that endeavor and you will impress your pet with the fact that you are in command during the grooming activity.

You should discourage your kitten from scratching furniture from the start. Training a kitten does not require corporal punishment. A stern "scat," accompanied by a clap of your hands is usually sufficient. Most kittens will quickly adapt to a scratching post that is kept near their beds. If a kitten persists in clawing furniture, you can enforce your "scat" with a squirt of water from a toy water gun.

Your Bengal will talk to you. As it grows and matures mentally, vocal communication is established between pet and owner. Certain sounds will be associated with particular circumstances. Besides the usual cat sounds, Bengals have been known to emit short barks and loud guttural purring that are very curious and enjoyable. However, if a kitten smells food and begins to rub on your leg, purr loudly, and utter a few meows, a bad habit is forming. When the kitten begins to sing for your supper, you need to act.

A cat's vocalization to gain attention or to beg for human food should be ignored and discouraged from the beginning of the human relationship. A tiny begging kitten is rather cute, but kittens grow up. An adult cat that cries loudly and gets under your feet in the kitchen, demanding tidbits, is annoying. Don't make the mistake of feeding your Bengal human food from the kitchen counter or from the dining table. It is best to physically confine your pet to another room while the human food is cooked, served, and eaten.

HOW-TO:
Protecting Your New Kitten

It is a good idea to confine your kitten for a short period when introduced into your home. Place the Bengal kitten's food and water dishes, its bed, a litter pan, and perhaps a scratching post in a small room. If a bathroom is used, be sure the toilet lid is kept down. Keep your kitten there continually for a few days, except when it is on your lap or in your arms. That restricted space gives the kitten a sense of security and protects it from injury while it is adapting to you.

When it is first allowed out of the room to investigate the rest of the home, watch it carefully. If your kitten can't be kept under close observation, return it to the confinement area until you have time to spend with it. Within a few days, after a dozen monitored excursions into the rest of the house, the Bengal will be comfortable in its new surroundings. At that time,

Insecticides present high risk to cats.

Hazards found in most homes.

move the food, water, and litter box to the areas you choose.

There are many hazards around the average home. A Bengal youngster is a curious, adventuresome little creature that will get itself into trouble if not watched. A new kitten in your home should stimulate your family to identify and eliminate dangers to its health.

• Balls of string, yarn, or thread present major hazards to a kitten. I have surgically retrieved threaded needles from the intestinal tract of many kittens. A swallowed length of string or thread, even without a needle, can be the cause of a surgical emergency. Be sure to remove the temptations. Put sewing baskets in a closed closet or on an unattainable shelf.

• Insecticides and household cleaning agents represent serious dangers to the kitten (see Poisoning, page 86).

• Older family pets often represent some danger to a kitten during the first month, and initially a kitten should be watched carefully when with other pets.

• Children may not realize how delicate a kitten's body is. Bengal kittens will soon learn to evade, escape, or defend themselves from young, uninformed children. In the introductory phase of child-cat relationships, don't leave a kitten and a small child together unattended. There is a particular reason for that advice: small, soft, furry, stuffed animals are often bought for babies. It may be cute to watch a toddler carry a stuffed kitten by one leg, squeeze it, bite its ears, or throw it on the floor and step on it. Unfortunately, when a small, soft, furry *real* kitten is brought home, a young child may not realize that the pet is a living being, and may treat it the

same way a stuffed animal is handled. A frightened kitten will strike back defensively if it is picked up by its tail, and both child and kitten are subject to injury.
• Pet doors present a major hazard to a kitten. They may allow a kitten to get outside, and the backyard fence will probably not contain a small kitten. Car tires may screech on the street in front of your home, and your Bengal may become a memory.
• Falling from high places is an ever present risk in Bengal homes. This risk is multiplied in apartments when cats are allowed roof or balcony access. Bengals love heights, but they

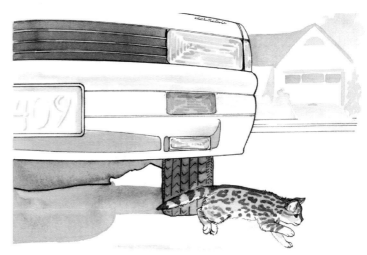

Automobiles present extreme risk to your pets.

Falling from high places is another hazard.

can be a serious hazard to your kitten's life.
• Open fireplaces attract kittens. They may be burned by glowing embers, and even if the fire is extinguished, the inquisitive kitten will probably track ashes all over your carpet.
• Certain houseplants present dangers to cats of all ages (see Poisoning, page 86).
• Irons, lamps, fans, radios, toasters, and other appliances may have electric cords, which attract playful kittens. Tugging on a cord may cause the kitten to pull the appliance from the table, possibly injuring itself and damaging the appliance.

Bengal kittens usually have an affinity for water. For a few months, it is a good idea to keep toilet lids closed. Hot tubs should be kept covered if the Bengal has access to them. A short swim might be harmless, but spas are not furnished with escape ramps for kittens.

The ultimate threat to a kitten's life is the great outdoors. Kittens that are allowed outside are at risk unless they are in your arms or on a leash. A neighborhood dog, car, bicycle, or skateboard can make short work of a kitten. Protect your pet's life and your investment. Keep your beautiful Bengal in the house!

Nutrition

During many years of association with cat owners, I have learned that few are interested in the technical data that usually accompanies a discussion of nutrition for their pets. Usually, cat owners want to get right to the bottom line, without wading through all of the calculations. Because your pet's diet is rarely formulated in the kitchen, little is served by lengthy discussions of essential amino acids, protein synthesis, enzyme functions, and vitamin activity. Pet food manufacturers often do the research and formulation, providing pet owners with the analysis and list of ingredients of the foods on the supermarket shelf, so that you can make your selections based upon palatability and nutritional value for your dollar spent.

A thorough scientific study of nutritional requirements for your cat, including the interaction of enzymes, hormones, and amino acid synthesis, is presented in *Nutrient Requirements Of Cats (Revised).* The book is available to you from the National Research Council (1-800-624-6242).

Water

Water is essential to sustain life. The nonfat component of mammalian bodies is about 73 percent water. It is available from liquids and solid foods. Canned cat food, for example, is 72 to 78 percent water. Water is also supplied in smaller quantities in semimoist diets that contain 25 to 35 percent, and appreciably less in dry cat foods that are 7 to 12 percent water.

Significant quantities of oxidation water are produced within the body by metabolism of carbohydrates, fats, and protein. Cats will typically drink water about the same number of times a day as they eat; they are very efficient in conserving water; and they can maintain normal health in the absence of drinking water when fed high moisture diets.

A constant source of water is extremely important in all cats' diets. Water intake is critical in aged animals or those under stress of illnesses. Ample drinking water is of foremost concern in pets suffering from conditions such as kidney compromise, diabetes, or hormonal disturbances.

Water is lost from the bodies of cats through their urine and feces. More is lost by evaporation from their respiratory tracts, mucous membranes of the eyes and mouth, and from the skin. Animals lose great amounts of water when they are suffering from digestive problems accompanied by diarrhea or vomiting. Lost water must be replaced constantly. Cats, like all intelligent beings, prefer fresh, clean drinking water.

Feeding Your Bengal

Cats are individuals by every definition of the word, but they have one thing in common. When a complete and balanced diet is offered, house cats will generally stop eating when their daily nutritional requirements are met. Bengals have mastered the art of nibbling and snacking. They will eat a dozen or more small meals a day, and will only gorge themselves if given access to large quantities of highly palatable foods.

Weigh your feline friend occasionally. Bengals are often heavier than they appear to be, due to their solid musculature and lack of soft fat. Adult cats require between 28 and 40 k/cal of energy, per pound of body weight per day, which means that a 10 pound (4.5 kg) adult cat should consume about 300 to 400 k/cal daily for maintenance.

An energetic young Bengal who climbs and exercises frequently, requires one fourth to one third more energy than one who is older and less active. The nutritional needs of pregnant queens, new mothers, and young kittens vary (see Breeding Your Bengal, beginning page 60).

The wide range of k/cal per ounce of the hundreds of cat foods presently available is mind-boggling, and the price range is equally broad. The price of a cat food does not necessarily reflect the nutritional value of the product. Packaging and advertising is included in the price.

The cost of each element used to produce a food that meets or exceeds your pet's daily requirements also affects the price of cat foods on the supermarket shelf. That's one reason why today's premium cat foods sit on one end of the price scale, and the generic foods on the other.

As is the case with most other manufactured food products, when you shop for cat food, you will usually get about what you pay for. Your Bengal's nutrition is a poor place to try to balance your household budget. House brands and generic packages may contain balanced nutrition, but their contents (and palatability) may vary as the prices of ingredients increase or decrease. It is also possible that a house brand may be identical to a brand-name product. Personal contact with manufacturers may reveal that information. Their addresses and phone numbers are usually easy to find on the packages.

Types of Cat Foods

The three types of prepared or formulated cat foods are: dry, semimoist, and canned. Protein digestibility ranges from 80 percent in dry cat foods, 85 percent in semimoist, and 90 percent in canned meat diets. Canned foods are usually about 75 percent water. Even though they contain meat, their formula may be only 10 percent protein, whereas a dry food with little or no animal products may contain 35 percent protein by dry weight.

Dry food: Although less energy-dense and less palatable, dry food has advantages that the other types do not share. It can be left unrefrigerated for free choice feeding. It is cleaner and easier to handle, and it usually costs less than the other two types.

Semimoist foods: These foods contain preservatives to prevent spoilage, and other elements are added to bind water. They are expensive, and feeding them frequently stimulates a significant increase in water consumption due to those chemical additives.

Canned foods: There are two varieties of canned foods: rations, which contain soy, cereal, meat, vitamins, and minerals, and gourmet foods, which contain more meat, vitamins and minerals, and less vegetable matter. Although a small rodent represents a balanced meal for a cat, a mouse is not all meat. Pure beef, pork, chicken, or fish are not balanced nutritionally. Other ingredients and supplements are included in canned formulations. Canned foods are expensive by comparison to dry foods. If the correct quantities are fed, however, spoilage is not a problem, because there should be no leftovers.

Cats have no actual fat requirement for energy. They can obtain all their energy from protein and carbohydrates. Fats add palatability to a food and some fat is needed for proper

The regal face of a Bengal cat.

storage and metabolism of fat-soluble vitamins (A, D, E, and K). Dry foods are lowest in fat; canned foods are highest. The range is from 9 to 20 percent. Wild felines' natural diets probably contain 40 percent fat, or even more, but that does not mean that you need to add fat to the diet of your house cat.

In the past, there was some fear about the high mineral content of cat foods, which was believed to cause feline urological syndrome (FUS). Research has shed much light on that disease, and today, most high-quality cat foods of all three types contain properly balanced minerals. Several are specially formulated to maintain an acidic urine production, minimizing the risk of FUS. Of the three types of food available, a premium canned variety is probably the food of choice in the prevention of FUS (see Noncontagious Diseases, page 82).

Premium brands of cat foods use a fixed formula that remains constant, even when the costs of ingredients change on the market. Some other less expensive foods use a least cost formula that results in variations in the ingredients used as the prices of those ingredients fluctuate. Unfortunately, unless you contact the manufacturer, you can't be sure what type of formula is used.

Read Labels

Labels can be misleading. When reading labels, always base your analysis on the dry matter weight. Each label is a legal document. If you want detailed information about cat food labels and label terminology, you can obtain a pamphlet (for a fee) from the Association of American Feed Control Officials (AAFCO) at 1-404-656-3637.

Some labels carry the important statement: *"Provides complete and*

Kitten playing hide and seek.

balanced nutrition for the growth and maintenance of cats as substantiated through testing in accordance with AAFCO feeding protocols." Take special note of that statement. When it is seen, the product can be fed as the only source of nutrition for kittens and adult Bengals.

If you want more information about the food, such as how the analysis was made, call or write to the manufacturer. The most valid analysis is obtained by animal feeding tests. That is primarily due to the fact that a laboratory analysis to establish compliance with AAFCO regulations does not necessarily address nutrient excesses, unmeasured toxic substances, or palatability.

Recipes for home-formulated diets are available in health food stores and libraries, and *Nutrient Requirements of Cats* gives some guidelines for formulating diets from natural ingredients.

Homemade diets should be avoided unless you can be sure of the protein, fat, and carbohydrate content, and the digestibility of every ingredient.

The age or shelf life of a product is another important consideration, especially in dry and semimoist products. After excessive storage time, some elements may be lost or rendered less nutritionally effective. For that reason, choose products that enjoy popularity among the cat owning public. For the same reason, purchase your Bengal's food from a busy store that has a high turnover of its products.

Supplements and Treats

There is no reason to supplement a Bengal's commercial, complete and balanced diet, but let's face it, you will probably treat your pet to something special once in a while. It is unlikely that your Bengal will be harmed in any

Read labels of cat foods.

way by being fed a treat occasionally. Take care not to furnish more than 20 percent of your cat's energy needs in the treats that you offer. Many cats enjoy cooked eggs (never feed raw egg whites), bits of cooked chicken, small amounts of cooked fish, or a bite of beef. If fed in small quantities, those products should cause no harm.

A better idea is to occasionally change the flavor (but not necessarily the brand) of the canned food you are using. Your feline buddy will appreciate a change now and then, and its diet will remain complete and balanced.

What Not to Feed

Table scraps: No matter how tempting, table scraps should never be substituted for cat food or used as treats. Feeding table scraps will stimulate nuisance behavior of cats when you are preparing or eating your meals. Table scraps are not complete and balanced meals for a cat. Human food seasonings and preservatives

such as benzoic acid may be toxic to your cat. It is speculated that propylene glycol, used in control of water activity in some processed human foods, may be detrimental to feline red blood cells.

Raw fish: In large quantities, raw fish will cause vitamin E deficiency in cats. Commercial feline diets that contain fish are supplemented with vitamin E. Products sold for human consumption, like canned tuna, are not complete, balanced diets for cats, and should not be used as a significant part of your Bengal's diet.

Milk: Milk is dangerous to feed, even in small quantities. Adult cats are usually deficient in lactase, the enzyme that digests the lactose sugar in milk. The composition of cow's milk is significantly different from cat's milk. When fed to kittens (and many adult cats), it will frequently cause diarrhea, resulting in dehydration, reduced activity, malnourishment, and depression.

Balanced vitamin and mineral supplements: Although these may not be harmful, if you are feeding a complete and balanced diet, they are a waste of money and have no nutritional value for the cat.

Liver: Containing high levels of vitamin A, liver may cause problems in any cat, especially kittens. It is also a laxative and is a very poorly balanced food.

Candy: Why anyone would feed candy to a cat is beyond comprehension, but in case you are thinking of it, don't! Most cats have no sweet tooth, they don't need sugar or nuts, and they certainly shouldn't have cocoa, which can be toxic to cats.

The Bottom Line

Cats' palates are not as sensitive as television commercials would lead you to believe. Bengals usually prefer their food at room temperature, not straight from the refrigerator, but they are not finicky eaters. They may be fed regular meals, once, twice, or three times a day, or they can be fed free choice dry food around the clock. Kittens need at least two, and preferably three or four, meals a day if no dry food is available to them during the day.

The best and most economical way to feed your adult Bengal is to purchase small packages of an excellent or premium quality dry food. If practical in your home, it may be fed free choice. In addition to the free choice dry food, offer half of a 6-ounce can of premium or excellent quality canned food each morning and evening for variety. Be sure that both the dry and canned foods contain the nutritional statement underlined above.

A 9 or 10 pound (4.1–4.5 kg) Bengal will maintain nicely on approximately 1/2 cup of dry food and one 6-ounce can of food a day, getting about half of its daily nutritional requirements from each of those two types of food. That combination should furnish about 300 k/cal. (For feeding recommendations for pregnant and lactating queens and their kittens, see Breeding Your Bengal, beginning page 60.)

There is no reason to change brands of food periodically. It is best to find one that agrees with both your pet and your purse, and stay with it. If you decide to change brands of food, it should not interfere with the cat's nutrition, providing that the change is made gradually, and the quality is maintained. Sudden changes often cause digestive upsets, so always add the new food to the old, in increasing amounts over a period of several days, while gradually reducing the old food.

Premium Brands

From the standpoint of the National Research Council's requirements, analysis, and compliance with AAFCO labeling, there is no particular reason for the added investment in premium foods. The increased cost of the pre-

Feeding free choice dry food is often best.

mium diets probably can't be justified when their formulas are compared to the formulas of the excellent quality brand-name products found in grocery stores. However, when premium foods are fed regularly, you might find that your Bengal simply looks better. Perhaps a feeding trial is in order, using your Bengal as the participant.

Selecting a Brand

Try feeding a specific grocery store cat food for three or four months. Keep a record of the cost of the food, *not* the quantity eaten. Then gradually change to a specific premium food that is purchased from a pet supply store or from your veterinarian. Record the cost of the premium food eaten over an equal period of time. Note which food the Bengal preferred, and try to evaluate the cat's condition and appearance. Then make your choice accordingly.

Living art.

Fat Cats

Obesity is not usually a problem with Bengals. If yours gains too much weight, stop free choice feeding and reduce its daily dietary intake by 15 or 20 percent until its weight has been reduced to the optimum. Many brands of cat food also offer a reduced calorie diet, specifically formulated to take weight off an obese cat while maintaining the complete and balanced formulation.

Avail yourself of the information that manufacturers will furnish about their foods. Write or call the producers of pet foods for specific analytic and feeding trial results. You will be amazed how much you can learn by comparing the various products by criteria other than the shelf price. The addresses and (sometimes free) telephone numbers are on the packages. Use them.

Grooming Your Bengal

Grooming your Bengal kitten may be a chore in the beginning, but it will soon become a pleasure enjoyed by both of you. Grooming is also one of the most important methods of communicating with your pet. It establishes a visual, vocal, and touch contact between you and your pet.

Cats are great groomers. They spend hours removing dead hair from their coats with their rough tongues. They lick their feet, and with dampened toes they clean their faces and ears. Unfortunately, young kittens are wont to play, nap, eat, then play again. They don't have time for serious grooming. Their mothers took care of that task until they were weaned, and as adults, grooming will again rise to importance.

During the interim period, their coats still need attention, and grooming becomes your responsibility by default. Even after maturity, when their personal grooming habit is established, cats are unable to reach certain areas of their anatomy with either tongues or feet. Nearly half of their bodies, including the entire dorsum or back, is not groomed unless another cat in the household pitches in.

Cats' licking is superficial. Their tongues do not reach the depths of healthy coats and dead hair is not adequately removed. The hair that you remove from your cat with a brush and comb won't be found on your clothes and furniture. Your identity as an ailurophile (cat lover) is confirmed by cat hair on your clothes, but that is a distinction that most of us will gladly forfeit.

Small tufts or mats of dry, dead hair make the cat look unkempt and dirty. Cats often scratch at those mats, causing skin irritation, pulling out healthy hair, and leaving bare patches. Your Bengal deserves better! Grooming the loose, dead hair from your pet's coat will also help to prevent the formation of hair balls in its stomach. They are sometimes vomited on your carpet, and although easy to clean up, they are easier to prevent. (See Hair ball [trichobezoar], page 83).

Bathing Your Bengal

Bengals are usually not afraid of water, so they may be easier to bathe than some other breeds, but bathing house cats is rarely necessary. Combing and brushing usually will keep their coats clean. If the kitten takes an expedition through fireplace ashes or some equally messy place, bathing is not difficult. First, trim its

Millwood *kittens.*

HOW-TO:
Grooming Tips

How to brush your Bengal.

Begin the comb and brush exercises the day your kitten arrives in your home. Grooming need not be a lengthy procedure, especially during the first few weeks, but it should be done regularly and frequently. Take care to use the comb and brush gently, and when finished grooming, spend a few minutes playing with the kitten.

If it is obvious that daily grooming is not necessary to maintain the healthy appearance of its coat, you can change the schedule to meet the needs.

Brushing and Combing

Brush and comb the coat in the direction of its grain. That is, from head to tail, and back to belly. Begin in an insensitive area such as the back of the neck and move over the entire body, including the tail and belly. If the cat grooms itself, concentrate your efforts on those areas that it cannot reach with its tongue.

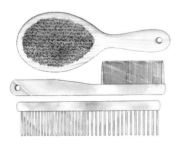

Essential grooming tools: comb, flea comb, and brush.

Initially you should hold your pet while grooming by gripping it from the underside of its chest, with its forelegs hanging down between your fingers. If needed, a gentle grip on the loose skin over the back of the neck may be used instead. Later, your kitten can be confined to your lap, on the floor between your legs, or on a table.

The cat comb will effectively remove the deep dead hair and will pluck out small tufts or mats if your delayed grooming schedule allows them to form. If fleas are indigenous to your area, a flea comb may be used on the cat's back and around the base of its tail to bring the flea dirt to the surface. That will help to identify the need for flea treatment. Brushing smoothes the coat after combing. Some of the rubber or soft, pliable plastic brushes on today's market do an excellent job of removing dead hair as well.

Ear Cleaning

If your kitten has a dirty face, ears, or feet, a damp wash-cloth may be used to sponge those areas clean. If a small quantity of ear wax is seen in

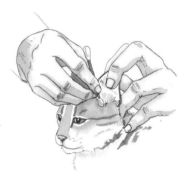

Gently swab outer ear canals.

the upper ear canals, it can be removed with a dry cotton swab. Do not reach deep into the ear canal with a cotton swab or any other tool. If your cat is scratching its ears and excessive, dark wax is found, have the ears examined for ear mites with an otoscope by your veterinarian. (See Otitis externa, page 84).

Care of Toenails

Some cats do not like to have their claws cut, and they become very obstreperous when their feet are held and their claws are extended. Because scratching posts are not always the perfect answer to furniture damage, it is essential that you cut your cat's claws. Usually, the procedure takes only a couple of minutes and needs to be repeated only every two or three weeks.

Until you and your Bengal become comfortable with the procedure, claw trimming is easiest if two people handle your pet. One holds the kitten while the other manages its foot and the nail trimmer. Use a trimmer that cuts cleanly, without crushing the nail. Hold a foot in one hand, with your thumb gently pressing the top of the knuckles. As pressure is applied to a toe knuckle, the

Best procedure for bathing your Bengal.

Watch for blood vessels when trimming nails.

claw will extend. The claw is pink at its toe attachment, and the sharp tip is transparent. In a bright light, the blood vessels within the nail are easy to see. They are pink and extend from the toe into the nail in a tapered, curved line. Slip the nail trimmer over the sharp tip of the nail, staying well ahead of the pink vessels.

If you cut too close to the vessels, you may see a drop or two of blood. That is rarely a serious problem. Before you start to trim the nails, place a dry bar of soap and a shaving (styptic) stick where they are handy. If a drop of blood is

seen, press the cut end of the bleeding nail into the dry bar of soap as if trying to scoop out some of the soap with the toenail, then hold the kitten for five minutes. Usually, the soap will stop the bleeding without further treatment.

If the bleeding continues, dampen the shaving stick with a few drops of water and press the dampened stick to the cut end of the nail, holding it there for a minute. Keep the kitten confined in a carrier or on your lap for 15 or 20 minutes after a bleeding nail has been treated, so that the bleeding will not start again.

nails to preserve the skin on your hands if your pet becomes frightened. The cat should be thoroughly combed and brushed before bathing because matted hair tends to be more difficult to remove when it is wet.

A two-compartment kitchen sink is very handy for bathing your Bengal. If not available, substitute two plastic dishpans that can be set side by side in your bathtub. It will be more convenient if your sink or tub has a spray

A cozy spot on a picture window sill—what more could a Bengal want?

attachment. If it does not, consider purchasing a removable sprayer hose to use. Put a rubber mat or a towel in the bottom of the sinks or pans and 4 or 5 inches (10–12.7 cm) of water at body temperature of 101 to 102° F (38.3–38.9°C) in each.

Pour a small amount of shampoo in the first sink. There are many good quality pet shampoos available. Flea and tick shampoos should not be used unless you are positive that the cat is infested with those parasites. Insecticides serve no useful purpose in an uninfested cat, and they may dry the skin. Stand the cat in the side of the sink that contains the shampoo, grasping it firmly but gently by the skin over the neck, close behind the head. With the other hand, dip soapy water onto the cat with your hand and work up a lather.

Do not attempt to lather the face and ears. Those areas are better cleaned later with a damp washcloth. After you have thoroughly lathered the body, transfer the cat to the other sink and rinse the coat well, using the sprayer. Hold the sprayer head tight against the cat, moving it all over the body. Be sure to keep the rinse water lukewarm, neither hot nor cold. Take care not to allow the sprayer to squirt the cat in the face.

Rinse the shampoo completely from the Bengal's coat to avoid skin irritation. If no sprayer is available, rinse the Bengal by dipping and pouring water over its body with your hand or a plastic cup, or from a 1-gallon (3.8 L) jug full of warm water that you set nearby.

A Bengal's coat dries quickly. Usually a brief rubdown with a towel is all that is required. Cats usually beat a hasty retreat when they are subjected to the noise of a hair dryer, although I have known a few laid-back Persians that didn't seem to mind them at all.

Bengals taking magnets off the refrigerator.

Showing Your Bengal

Who Can Be Shown?

If you have a show cat, or if you plan to breed your Bengal, you are obviously interested in cat shows. Even if your registered Bengal was purchased as a pet, it can be shown if it has Stud Book status. All registered Bengals that have three generations of registered Bengals in their background may be shown. If you believe that your pet Bengal deserves to be exhibited, and if it meets the show criteria, there is no reason not to show it. Of course there is absolutely no assurance that it will win a ribbon or title, but showing a pet is a valuable experience in itself. A cat show is a fun way to spend a weekend, to look at the finest specimens of your favorite breeds, and to meet other Bengal fanciers.

Household Pet classes are gaining popularity year by year. There is as much excitement and competitive spirit among pet class cat owners as among established cat breeders in championship classes. In TICA shows, household pet winners receive not only ribbons and honors among their peers, they also earn titles comparable to breeding cat classes. They compete for Master, Grand Master, Double, Triple, Quad, and Supreme Grand Master titles. In addition to ribbons and titles, the winners are given recognition in the yearbook and at the regional and international awards ceremonies.

Before you make a cat show commitment, have your Bengal faulted by an experienced breeder and exhibitor. He or she can help you decide whether or not to spend your time and money on a cat show entry. If the consensus is that your Bengal can stand up in some measure to current competition, go for it. Remember that colors, patterns, and conformation are not the only things that are judged in show rings.

If you aren't taking excellent care of your cat, show exhibition will probably be a disappointment. A cat in poor physical condition or one that is not well groomed has little chance of being "put up" in competition. A judge may look beyond its best qualities and only see the evidence of a poor diet or grooming.

If you plan to show your Bengal in the kitten class (four to eight months old), consider another point. Unless it is outstanding, a very young animal will rarely win against one that is three or four months older. Also remember that the period before six months of age is

Cats are judged individually.

The winner.

If you have not yet attended a cat show, now is the time to correct that oversight. Only attending a show in person can give you the feeling of excitement that is alive in the show hall. You will discover a couple of hundred cats and their owners, cages everywhere, and at least five or six judging rings in use at the same time. To the novice, it is utter chaos, but actually, cat shows are well organized. Take a day off from your routine and go to one, if only as a spectator. Arrive early in the morning, buy a catalog, and follow an experienced exhibitor around through the maze of cages and people. Whether or not your Bengal is entered, it will be a day well spent.

the most susceptible time for contracting contagious diseases. Be sure your Bengal is up-to-date on vaccinations!

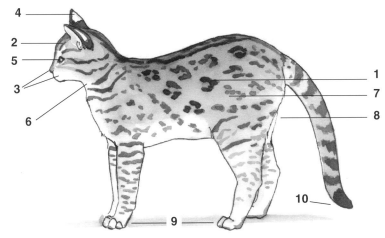

Study the Bengal standard before selecting a kitten.

1. Coat pattern and markings: Distinct horizontally aligned or random spots in extreme contrast to background color. Rosettes very desirable. No vertical stripes. Spotted belly. Bold chin-strap and mascara markings desirable.
2. Bridge of nose extends above eyes.
3. Broad muzzle, prominent whisker pads.
4. Medium small ears, rounded tips.
5. Large, oval, wide set eyes.
6. Proportionately long, thick, muscular neck.
7. Muscular legs and torso.
8. Hind legs slightly longer than front.
9. Large, round feet.
10. Tail thick and tapered, round very dark tip.

Quadruple grand champion Windstorm Solar Night *with raccoon.*

TICA Bengal Standard

Only a few of the general aspects of the Bengal standard follow. A complete standard may be obtained from The International Cat Association (TICA) (see Cat Associations, page 91).

General description: The goal of the Bengal breeding program is to create a domestic cat that has physical features distinctive to the small forest-dwelling wild cats, but with the loving, dependable, temperament of the domestic cat. Keeping this goal in mind, judges shall give special merit to those characteristics in the appearance of the Bengal that are distinct from those found in other domestic cat breeds.

Conformation: The conformation gives the Bengal cat a basic feral appearance. It is medium to large, sleek, and very muscular with hindquarters slightly higher than the shoulders. The head is a broad modified wedge with rounded contours, longer than it is wide, with a large nose and prominent whisker pads. The ears are medium set, medium small, short, with a wide base and rounded tips.

Patterns: *The spotted pattern:* Spots shall be random, or aligned horizontally. Rosettes formed by a part-circle of spots around a distinctly redder center are preferable to single spotting, but not required. Contrast with ground color must be extreme, giving a distinct pattern and sharp edges. A strong, bold chin strap and mascara markings are desirable. Blotchy horizontal shoulder streaks are desirable. The belly must be spotted.

The marbled pattern: Markings, while derived from the classic tabby gene, shall be uniquely different with as little bull's-eye similarity as possible. The pattern shall, instead, be random giving the impression of marble, preferably with a horizontal flow when the cat is stretched. Vertical striped mackerel influence is also desirable. Preference should be given to cats with three or more shades; i.e., ground color, markings, and dark outlining of those markings. Contrast must be extreme, with distinct shapes and sharp edges. The belly must be spotted.

Temperament: The temperament must be unchallenging. Any sign of definite challenge shall disqualify. The cat may exhibit fear, seek to flee, or generally complain aloud, but may not threaten to harm. Bengals should be confident, alert, curious, and friendly cats.

Show Tips

Should you decide to exhibit your registered Bengal, start the procedure by telephoning the entry clerk. The name of the clerk of a nearby show can be obtained from the various Bengal associations, TICA, or magazine ads (see Useful Addresses and Literature, page 91). The clerk will furnish entry forms, the time and place of the show, directions to the hall, and information about the availability of litter, litter pans, and food.

A cat will not be judged if it appears ill or has congenital faults such as polydactylia (extra toes), tail faults, malocclusion of the jaws, or is unruly or pregnant. (Congenital faults are not penalized in the alter classes.) If your Bengal is soon due for vaccination boosters, have them done at least two weeks before showing. If the entry clerk advises you that rabies vaccination is required, be sure to take the rabies certificate with you.

If your grooming program is on schedule, it is probably not necessary to bathe your cat before a show. A judge can refuse to handle a cat if it is dirty, but bathing your Bengal immediately before a show may leave the coat undesirably fluffy. Clip the nails of all four feet before a show.

Wade through the show rules, and enlist the aid of an exhibitor friend when filling out your first entry form. Be especially careful that the class information you furnish is correct. The categories are sometimes confusing but they are well defined in the rules. The show may last one or two days, and your cat may be shown five or six times each day. If you decide to ask an experienced exhibitor to stand in for you on show day, be sure that person is listed on the entry form as your agent. The number of cats entered in a show is limited, so to assure your place in the exhibition hall, don't procrastinate. After you send in the entry fee with the completed entry form, you

Leopard female watching TV.

will receive a confirmation of your entry within days. Be sure to check all data on the confirmation, and if any errors are found, call the clerk.

Benching Your Bengal

Upon arrival at the show hall, a clerk will furnish your cat's entry number and assign it a cage. You will receive a catalog and other information pertinent to the show hall and the show itself. You confine your cat to its preassigned, numbered cage where it will remain for the day except when you groom it or when it is being judged in a show ring.

Most cages are divided, with one cat in each side. Your Bengal might be more comfortable occupying both sides of the double cage at its first show. That can be arranged with the clerk. Cats remain in the cages until the judge calls your breed and class to the judging ring.

Certain rules and customs must be followed when outfitting your cage. Bench cages must be covered on three sides, but most handlers also cover the top. The covers need be nothing more than a set of bath towels held to the cage by safety pins or spring clips, but they are frequently more elaborate. You will see them beautifully hand embroidered, tasseled, and ornately decorated, resembling the bed curtains of an Eastern prince. Some type of soft bedding is needed for the bottom of the cage. A towel will suffice, but everything from upholstered couches to satin or velvet bean bags are seen in the cages.

Occasionally, the show committee may allow owners to furnish their own cages. If you desire to do so, be sure to discuss it with the clerk, because there may be restrictions.

If you are uncomfortable with the prospect of exhibiting your Bengal the first time, make a note on your entry form asking to be benched near a

Cat Show Equipment
- cage curtains or bath towels
- a dozen large safety pins or spring clips
- brush and comb
- small, dampened chamois cloth
- treats such as strained chicken
- small fold-up wooden TV table for grooming
- pad for grooming table (thick place mat or towel)
- three or four disposable litter pans
- food and water dishes
- thermos of fresh drinking water from home
- spray bottle of favorite disinfectant
- roll of paper towels
- small supply of usual cat food

friend who is also showing. If you ask, most shows will lend extra guidance to novice handlers as well.

Show Necessities

There are a few important items to take to the show with you. Some shows furnish litter and litter pans, but if your cat is finicky about the type of litter used, better take your own. The same applies to food and water. They may be available at the show, but there is no guarantee that your pet's favorite food will be there, or that the water will taste like your Bengal's usual supply.

Safety pins or spring clips are needed to fasten cage curtains and secure any loose joints in the cage. A small grooming table is convenient but not essential. Take a disinfectant to use on the cage, tables, and other items that may need cleaning.

Transportation to the Show

The heavy, fiberglass carrying kennel (see Transporting Your Kitten, page 38) is preferable. If a long trip is necessary to get to the show, put a small disposable litter tray in the kennel with your cat. If not, try using an extra large disposable diaper in the bottom of the transportation cage. It will serve as soft bedding, and if an accident occurs, it is easy to clean up. Some carrying kennels have small spill-proof water pans in them. If not, water can be provided before leaving home and when you stop. At the show, water can be left with the cat in the bench cage, or it can be offered periodically throughout the day. Food should be offered during the day as well, but many cats will only eat in the evening, when settled into a quiet motel room.

Judging Categories

Several different judges work independently in perhaps six separate rings in the show hall. Each judging event is handled autonomously by the judge in that ring. Cats that are entered in the show are qualified to be judged in every ring. Each judge awards separate ribbons for each class. There are both specialty and all-breed judges. The distinctions are explained in the show rules. The categories established in cat shows are:
• Championship (unaltered adults, eight months old or older)
• Altered (adults that have been neutered or spayed)
• Kittens (between the ages of four and eight months)
• New Breed and Color or Provisional (breeds or colors that have not been accepted for championship showing)
• Household Pets (must also be altered)
• Household Pet Kittens

Exhibiting your Bengal requires patience. Eventually, your cage number will be called to a show ring for judging. When carrying your Bengal from the benching cage to and from the ring cage, be sure to hold your pet with a firm grip, using both arms to cradle the cat close to your body. A loose cat in a show hall is very disconcerting to everyone, and is frowned upon by the officials who often get testy with the person responsible for the escapee. Once you have deposited your charge in its ring cage, given it a quick swipe with the chamois and a reassuring speech about your love (even if it doesn't win), take your seat in the audience. The rest is up to the judge.

Judging of each cat is very brief, taking only a minute or two. The judge handles the cat, compares it to the breed standard, and after seeing every cat in the class, the awards are made. Certain cats will be called back to the judging ring at a later time for the final judging of the best of each breed against each other. Be sure to pay close attention to the announcements that are made over the P A system and on chalkboards around the hall.

One final word about showing. Your time and expense for a show represent the cost of discovering how a particular set of judges compare your Bengal to the breed standard and to the other cats that are entered in the same class on a particular day. All judges do not agree on every cat in a show. They might even place the same cats differently in another show on another date.

Breeding Your Bengal

If you own a breeding-quality queen that has reached at least a year of age, and if you are considering breeding her, first examine your motives for doing so.

Breeding your Bengal for any reasons other than to improve and perpetuate the established characteristics of the breed is wrong. The joy of breeding Bengals should not be restricted to an elite few, but you must be prepared to research the genetics involved with selection of a mate, to

Professional examinations are essential.

care for your queen during pregnancy, to assist in delivery if necessary, to properly care for the kittens, and to locate suitable homes for them.*

Your responsibility to the Bengal breed and to the community does not end when a nice litter of kittens is produced. Your work has only just begun.

One of the poorest motives for breeding your Bengal queen is to make money. If that is your objective, speak to a Bengal breeder about it. You may be surprised.

Producing kittens from pet-quality females and pet-quality males is detrimental to the breed. In any breed, especially one as new as the Bengal, many pet kittens are produced by dedicated breeders who are striving to improve the breed. Even in the most carefully planned litters, a small percentage of the kittens is of breeding or show quality.

Assuming that you have a fine female Bengal, one that exceeds the minimum standards, and has proven her quality in show rings, the following discussion will help you plan and carry out your breeding program.

Breeding Capability

There is a saying among veterinarians that goes: An adult queen is spayed, is in season, or is pregnant. Bengal queens begin their estrous (heat) cycles between six and nine months of age, and each heat period

---

*In my years of veterinary practice I found that the most common reason for breeding a queen was "to teach the children about the miracle of birth, and to let them watch the kittens grow." That doesn't sound all bad on the surface, but unfortunately, the teaching session only lasts a few weeks. I was too often involved with euthanasia of abandoned kittens that wound up in shelters, pounds, and alleys. I am a devout advocate of family planning of the pet population.

lasts one to two weeks. Unlike dogs, female cats do not produce a bloody vaginal discharge or swelling of the external genitalia when in heat. According to most texts, queens begin their estrous cycles in the early spring and cease to cycle in the fall, but don't count on it! There is certainly some correlation between the season of the year and the estrous cycles of a cat, but experience has shown that many female cats, especially those living in moderate climates and those that are kept inside homes, continue to cycle year-round. Lots of kittens are delivered in February.

Following their very obvious estrus, females typically go out of heat and remain quiet during metestrus for perhaps a week or two. Then the active signs of estrus begin again. The physical and vocal signs that announce a queen in heat are impossible to miss (see Choosing the Sex, Females, page 30.)

Female Bengals should be at least one year of age before they are bred, although their heat cycles begin at about six months of age. Pregnancies before maturity can have a devastating effect on the health of the queen.

Examinations and Vaccinations

Two to four weeks before breeding your queen, visit your health care professional. A physical examination is advised, and a stool sample should be taken to the vet to have her checked for internal parasites. At about the same time, she should be vaccinated for several common feline diseases. Those vaccinations are critically important to protect her health, and to assure that her antibody level is at a peak when the kittens are born. The litter will receive a significant passive or temporary immunity from the antibodies that are obtained from the queen's colostral milk.

Locating a Mate

No matter how nearly perfect your queen is, her offspring will reflect the genes of the tom as well. For this reason, it is important to find a mate that complements her best qualities. The breed is too new to have all the wrinkles ironed out of the complex genetic fabric from which the Bengal is woven. A great deal of study is being done on that subject.

At the present time, experienced breeders who participated in developing the Bengal are your best source of information on how to choose a mate for your queen. They have discovered some of the secrets of compatibility between the various Bengal bloodlines. Take advantage of their experience. Join a Bengal club, subscribe to its newsletter (see Bengal Breed Clubs, page 92), and talk with knowledgeable breeders that you meet at cat shows.

A single stud can be responsible for producing several hundred kittens a year, whereas a female will probably produce less than two litters in the same period of time. A stud cat is proven worthy to use by show awards and by the quality of his progeny. Personality and manners are hereditary, to a great extent. Your choice of a sire for your new Bengals should include consideration of the quality of his existing offspring, especially if some are from females related to your queen.

Critically evaluate the queen and the prospective mates and their pedigrees. Choose the most likely candidate and arrange with his owner for the mating when your queen next comes into season. When that perfect mate is chosen, and the breeding time and place are agreed upon, set your sights realistically. Do not expect a large litter of perfect kittens, all of which will be of show winning quality. If you have made your selection of a mate prudently, and if your queen is excep-

Vaccinations are very important.

tional, perhaps one or two kittens of the litter will be of that quality.

Stud owners charge for the services of their cats, and there are written agreements to be signed by the owners of both the male and female, prior to mating them. These documents may be important when the time comes to register and sell the kittens.

The Right Time to Breed

Technically, a female ovulates and can conceive on a single mating and on the first day she shows signs of heat. Her ovulation is stimulated by coitus, and from that standpoint, it is hard to miss the right time for mating.

In a controlled breeding program, it is more prudent to leave the pair together, separated from other animals and humans, for an entire day or two. The most productive time of mating is sometime between the second and fifth day of her visible heat signs.

Cats will mate several times a day, and the probability of conception increases with repeated matings. On occasion, a male may be overly aggressive, and a queen may be injured if they are left together unmonitored for extended periods. In those cases, you should kennel one of the

pair, preferably the male, except during the actual matings.

Bengals are not problem breeders, and only rarely will an adult queen fail to exhibit discernible signs of estrus. If your queen has reached one year of age without showing the obvious signs of heat, and if she is normal on physical examination, she may have silent or unapparent heat cycles. The best way to deal with that problem is to house her with an experienced male for a month during the late spring or early summer. Between the two of them, they will decide when the best time is to mate.

If an experienced tom is being used, the place of breeding is somewhat irrelevant. If it is the first mating for your queen, and if the male's owner agrees, you may wish to bring the tom to the queen. He is more likely to be aggressive, and she will be less shy in familiar surroundings. Please note that owners of breeding toms may not turn their valuable Bengal studs over to you without restrictions. All breeding toms come equipped with foul smelling spraying habits with which you must contend if you bring one into your home.

A gentle, formal introduction of the tom is advisable. To accomplish that, cage the male and allow the queen to approach him, beginning the mating prelude through the bars of the kennel. After about an hour, open the kennel and observe.

The cats' mating ritual is not a proceeding that wants human intervention. Occasionally, the mating will take place as soon as you open the male's cage. Sometimes however, a measure of feline decorum demands privacy. In case the pair do not approach each other in your presence, leave the room, and watch them through a window or a cracked door.

If the breeding area is tiled or some other slick floor surface prevails, provide a big throw rug. A surface providing good traction is very desirable to accomplish the mating ritual with the least difficulty.

The Mating Act

As is the case with many other team projects, more predictable results are achieved when the male or female, or both, are experienced in the mating game. A young tom that has not yet sired a litter will probably perform adequately with your virgin queen, but an experienced tom would be preferable.

Don't be surprised at the moaning, yowling, and other cries that emanate from the tom and queen. Cats are usually quite vocal during mating. The male will usually court his mate with low guttural sounds for a few minutes, then he will grasp the female's dorsal neck skin in his teeth. That act often precipitates some sounds of anguish from the queen. He will quickly mount her from the side, stepping on her hind leg while maintaining his hold on the skin of her neck. In response to his rough but amorous advances, the female holds her tail to one side and points her posterior upward. In a few seconds, as he finalizes his role in the reproductive act, the female will emit a reverberating howl that is hard to miss if you are in the same neighborhood.

As painful as it all sounds, the couple is usually anxious to repeat the performance in two or three hours. After a few matings have been observed, mark your calendar. In 63 days, kittens should arrive.

Aftercare of the Queen

The level of hormones causing the heat signs do not instantly disappear when mating occurs. You can expect the female to continue to show mild signs of heat for a few days. Her appetite and personality should return to normal within a day or two after the stress of estrus and breeding is over.

After mating, the female will usually have some scratches on the top of her neck, left by his incisors. After the last mating, dampen the hair of the area with alcohol and examine the skin carefully. The male's tooth marks are usually superficial and rarely cause any problems. They should be left alone to scab and heal. Puncture wounds that extend through the skin are rarely the result of mating, but if any penetrations are noted, they should be examined and treated by your health care professional.

Gestation

The average time of pregnancy in domestic cats, including Bengals, is 63 days. The published gestation range for all cats is from 59 to 65 days. Those numbers should not be engraved in gold. Most veterinarians who took x-rays of normal pregnant queens on their sixty-fifth, sixty-eighth, or even seventieth day of gestation, soon learned that the procedure was hardly ever necessary. If the queen continues to eat and act normally, and no foul vaginal discharge is noted, she will very likely deliver her kittens by her own calendar, irrespective of veterinarian charts and predictions.

The earliest that pregnancy can be affirmed is between 15 and 20 days. At that time, an experienced veterinarian can discern the tiny, nodular fetuses by abdominal palpation with practiced fingers. That procedure should not be attempted by someone who is inexperienced in proper technique. At about four weeks' gestation, some abdominal enlargement will be noted, and usually the nipples will begin to appear more prominent. Near the delivery date, queens will often pluck out patches of hair surrounding their nipples.

If the expectant queen stops eating, has an elevated temperature, becomes depressed, and licks at her genitalia excessively during pregnancy, she and her kittens may be in

Windstorm Sacajewea, *female leopard kitten.*

trouble and require medical or surgical intervention. Note the expected date of delivery on your calendar as a reference point, but don't get terribly excited if the kittens arrive a few days on either side of the predicted date.

Changes in the Queen

If your pregnant Bengal is fed with free access to an excellent or premium quality cat food, there is no reason to change or to add supplements to her diet. By the third or fourth weeks of pregnancy, her appetite will gradually increase until shortly before parturition (delivery). During gestation, her food intake will be at least 25 percent higher than her maintenance level. A queen normally weighing 7.5 pounds (3.4 kg) will probably weigh nearly 11 pounds (5 kg) at delivery time. She should continue to be active and playful for at least six of her nine weeks of gestation. The last two or three weeks, as her abdomen becomes pendulous and turgid, her activity will decrease.

As the time for parturition nears, you can expect your outgoing, affectionate Bengal to become somewhat reclusive. She will seek out some secluded place and spend more time away from your family than normal. She may also become more possessive of that place of refuge. During the last two weeks of gestation, when she lies on her side, you can observe the fetuses changing positions. It is OK to gently lay your palm on her abdomen to feel the activity of the kittens, but to invite strangers to do so is not a good idea. An expectant mother may be more loving than usual toward her favorite people, and at the same time she may resent the attentions of children, pets, and strangers.

The Maternity Ward

As the expectant queen becomes more reclusive, provide a room or a large wire cage for her that is off-limits to children and other pets. That maternity room should be equipped

Stalking tactics.

with her litter pan, food, water, and a nesting box.

The nesting box need be nothing more elaborate than a "cave" fashioned from an enclosed cardboard carton with a "door" opening in one end. The size of her box should be large enough to allow the queen to stretch out in any direction and to accommodate her and her brood. At the same time, it should be small enough to confine the infant kittens within reach of their mother. A box with a top, that is more or less 2 feet (0.6 m) square and 1 foot (0.3 m) tall, with a 6-inch (15.2 cm) hole cut in one end about 3 inches (7.6 cm) from the floor is adequate.

Pillows or loose towels or blankets should not be used in the nest box. Avoid all bedding material that might allow a kitten to crawl under and separate itself from its mother and siblings. The best surface is one that is soft and flat, and that extends from wall to wall in the box. A piece of clean, short-nap carpet cut to fit the bottom of the box is ideal. Stretch a towel over the carpet and tuck it tightly beneath the carpet around the edges. Avoid nesting materials that are shaggy or ones that have a nap that might produce bits of fuzz that can be a source of trouble for the kittens.

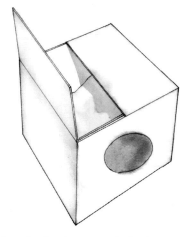

A nesting box is a very private place.

HOW-TO:
Assisting in Delivery

When it is obvious that the dam needs help, render the assistance as quickly as possible, then return the kitten to its mother.

A kitten may partially emerge from the birth canal, then remain there. If a kitten remains in that position without progress for more than three or four minutes, you should act. With clean hands, using a dry washcloth, pinch and tear the membranes that cover the kitten's head, and gently wipe the membranes away from its face and from its mouth. Then watch closely for progress.

If the kitten remains extended from the birth canal without progress for another three or four minutes, more assistance should be rendered. With a dry cloth, grasp the kitten's head and shoulders carefully, and apply gentle traction.

The mother begins cleaning the newborn kittens immediately.

The direction of traction is very important. A normal birth canal is tipped downward, and traction is most effective if exerted in a direction nearly parallel to the dam's pelvic canal. To understand that concept, picture her standing up. The appropriate direction of traction would be toward the floor at a point three or four inches (7.6–10 cm) in back of her hind feet.

Once you have extracted the kitten from the birth canal, quickly remove any remaining membranes from its head and swab the fluid and mucus from its mouth with a corner of the washcloth or apply light suction to the mucus by aspirating with a syringe. If the newborn is squirming and breathing, place it in front of the dam and step back; she will finish cleaning the kitten. Kittens' first breaths are always short gasps and are no cause for alarm.

Another situation that occasionally requires assistance is a very rapid delivery. Once in a while, kittens are born in such quick succession that the mother does not have time to clean and care for them adequately. In that case, your help may be very important. Pick a kitten up with a cloth and clean the membranes from its head and mouth with the dry washcloth as described above, then place it in front of the dam with the placental membranes still attached.

A kitten that has fluid retained in its lungs or upper respiratory system could need your assistance. It may have been in the birth canal for a

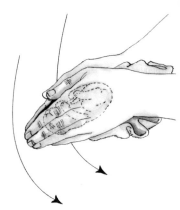

Kitten in trouble: Swing in wide arc.

long period, or it may be the victim of a rapid delivery and insufficient attention of the mother cat. Newborn kittens normally obtain their first air in short gasps, but if a kitten is observed gasping or blowing mucus bubbles from its nose for several minutes, it may need help.

Use a washcloth to pick up and cradle the kitten in your upturned palms. Hold it so that its belly is up and its head is away from you and supported between your two index fingers. Hold your thumbs over its chest in a gentle, firm grip. Then, standing with your feet apart and your arms extended, swing the kitten in a wide arc beginning from the height of your waist. The arc ends between your legs, near the floor, behind your feet.

The swinging action creates centrifugal force that extrudes fluids from the kitten's lungs and upper respiratory tract. After two swings, wipe its nostrils, swab out its mouth with a corner of the cloth, and gently massage its chest for a moment or two. Repeat the procedure until the bubbling stops and the kitten is breathing normally. Usually once or twice is adequate.

If the kitten does not breathe after the above procedure is repeated two or three times, prop its mouth open with a finger, and from a distance of several inches, blow into its mouth. If the kitten still does not breathe, repeat all the procedures again. Continue these CPR efforts for at least a half hour, or until it is obvious that the kitten will not respond.

The Placenta

If the mother cat chews through the umbilical cords within a short time after birth, no human attention is needed. If she leaves the placenta attached to the kittens for more than an hour, you may wish to assist. Clamp the cord about 1 inch (2.5 cm) from the kitten's belly with a hemostat (see Supplies for Kitten Delivery,

Bengal newborn nursing from bottle.

Mother aids in delivery of kitten.

page 68). Cut the cord between the hemostat and the placenta with a pair of sterile scissors, and dip the kitten's end of the severed cord in a vial of disinfectant. Leave the hemostat clamped to the cord for at least ten minutes. It is normal but not necessary for the dam to eat some placentas, but if she consumes too many they may cause diarrhea or vomiting.

Breach or Posterior Births

Many kittens are born head first, but posterior presentations of the tail and hind legs are not uncommon. The significance of a posterior birth is that the kitten's head is the last to arrive, and the placenta may be detached from the uterus before its head emerges. In that event, quick delivery is imperative. If a kitten's tail and hind legs protrude from the birth canal for three or four minutes without complete delivery, apply traction. The procedure is the same as described above except that traction is applied on the hind legs and pelvis of the kitten instead of its head. Be gentle!

A true breach birth is not common. In a mature queen it is not necessarily cause for alarm, but it does deserve your undivided attention. In a breach presentation, only the tail of a kitten emerges from the birth canal. The hind legs are tucked forward in the birth canal, and are not visible or accessible. Many such presentations proceed at a normal pace, and no intervention is necessary. However, if only a tail is apparent and the birth process is at a standstill for more than ten minutes, call your vet immediately. Do not attempt to deliver a breach kitten by applying traction to the tail only.

Detecting Delivery Problems (Dystocia)

Dystocias or difficult births that should cause you to contact your Bengal's veterinarian immediately include nonproductive labor or a lengthy interruption of labor. If the queen shows signs of abdominal labor for an hour without producing a kitten, call the veterinarian. If she delivers part of the litter, but there are obviously more to come, and she stops labor for more than two hours, call the vet. If there is blood coming from her birth canal, get to the phone. The presence of a foul-smelling green or black discharge before the first kitten is born is another reason for phoning the veterinarian. (Note, however, that after the birth of the first kitten, a greenish fluid is normal.)

Windstorm Kara Mia *and leopard kittens.*

Supplies for Kitten Delivery
• a supply of old washcloths that have been laundered and rinsed well
• two or three pairs of "mosquito" hemostat forceps (surplus store or pet supply store)
• a pair of straight, blunt surgical scissors (pet supply or surplus store)
• a small bottle of umbilical cord disinfectant such as organic iodine (as recommended by your Bengal's veterinarian)
• a new sterile 3cc syringe (pet supply store or your veterinarian can supply)

When early signs of labor are seen, boil the metal instruments in a shallow, covered pan of water for 15 minutes to render them free of germs, then pour the water off and keep the dry instruments in the covered pan. Put a tablespoon of the disinfectant solution in a small container such as a 1-ounce measuring cup that may be used to dip umbilical cords.

Signs of Labor
An expectant mother will sometimes give you ample warning that labor is approaching; sometimes she won't. A two- or three-degree Fahrenheit drop in her body temperature is a fairly accurate way to predict parturition. If you take her rectal temperature every eight hours, when it drops from the normal of 101.5°F (38.7°C) to 98 or 99°F (36.7–37.2°C), look for kittens within eight to 12 hours.

The earliest outward signs of impending labor are reduced appetite, restlessness, abnormal breathing, pacing, and frequent trips to her nest box. If she stays in her bed, licks at her genitalia persistently, changes her position frequently, and seems uncomfortable, early labor has probably begun. A clear, mucoid, odorless vaginal discharge is usually apparent at that time. Delivery may begin within minutes or a few hours after those signs are observed.

If a green, black, bloody, or foul-smelling discharge is seen before the arrival of the first kitten, call your veterinarian.

It is common for a queen to show preliminary signs of labor, then appear normal for a few hours, then begin labor in earnest. Productive labor signs are very obvious. The queen lies on her side, and abdominal muscle contractions progress from mild to very strong. Her abdomen becomes taut as she applies muscular pressure. Then some fluid will emerge from the vaginal tract, followed by almost transparent placental membranes, and a kitten is on the way!

Parturition
Queens in good health, especially Bengals, do not often need help during their delivery of kittens. Usually, you may seek out the queen some morning only to discover a beautiful litter of babies contentedly nursing or squirming about the nest. If you are fortunate enough to witness the birth of kittens, you will be amazed at the instinctive knowledge and ability that a

Junglebook *litter, showing spotting at 12 weeks.*

new mother cat possesses.

Unnecessary human intervention in a normal kitten delivery may cause several problems that can be avoided if the queen is simply allowed to do that which she is capable of and willing to do. Bengals are especially independent in giving birth! Allow the queen to take care of every aspect of parturition if the delivery progresses in a productive manner. The pace or speed of delivery is irrelevant if she is producing live kittens and cleaning them, and none appears to be having difficulty breathing.

During and immediately following parturition, do not handle the kittens more than is necessary. Bengals are the best mothers imaginable, and only on rare occasions will they abandon a kitten or a litter. When they do, it may be due to excessive human intervention in the delivery process. There is a rare but ever present possibility that the mother cat will abandon a kitten that has been cleaned, dried, and handled excessively by the owner at the time of birth.

A Bengal kitten is usually born in one fluid motion, propelled from the queen's womb by uterine and abdominal muscle contractions. Sometimes, kittens are born in stages. As a kitten's head emerges from the queen's birth canal, the queen might turn and grasp it, tearing the membranes from its head. She may pull on the kitten to assist in delivery.

Each kitten is contained within its own placental sac. Each kitten's placenta detaches from the uterus and is shed within minutes after the kitten is born. Retained placentas are rare in domestic felines, but if possible, count the placentas as they are produced, to be sure that they number the same as the kittens in the litter. Placental retention, if it does occur, may be a source of uterine infection, and if suspected, you should contact your veterinarian.

Once it is free of the birth canal, she will lick the membranes from the kitten's face and body, drying it and massaging its chest, as she rolls it over and over. When the kitten's placenta is

Nursery box to confine kittens for a few weeks.

Neonatal Kitten Care

Within the confines of the maternity nest, kittens are tough, aggressive little critters. It is not uncommon to see them nursing while their umbilical cords are still attached to placentas. At the age of two or three hours, they respond to the dam's voice and touch, fighting their ways to the sources of her warm nourishing milk. Of all the species that I have had the pleasure of ministering to, I have found the cat to be incomparable as a mother. The proud, purring Bengal dam, curled around her brood of fat little kits sleeping in a spotted heap, is a picture of contentment that is truly unforgettable.

For the first couple of weeks of life, she cleans, grooms, and nurses the kittens most of the time that she is not attending to her own nutritional and excretory needs. She licks their abdominal and urogenital areas, stimulating them to excrete and consuming their excretions. She examines them several times daily, methodically sorting out the ones that need grooming or cleaning the most. For this reason, among others, the best way to care for the daily needs of a litter of newborn kittens is to assure the good health and nutrition of their mother throughout her life, but especially from the time of breeding until the kittens are weaned.

Determining the Sex of Your Kittens

View the neonatal kittens from the rear, with their tails elevated. The aperture of the female genitalia is immediately below her anus. The opening into the male prepuce is similar in appearance, but it is much lower, more distant from his anus. The testicles may not be discernible at birth, but within a week they can be seen and felt in the space between the anus and the prepuce orifice.

shed from her uterus, she will chew the umbilical cord in two, often eating the placenta as she does so. When she is satisfied that all is in order with that kitten, if another is not yet presented, she may push the kitten to a nipple and encourage it to nurse.

The time lapse between births ranges from a few minutes to an hour or two. There is no cause for alarm unless the queen is in hard labor for an hour without producing a kitten. If that occurs, call your veterinarian.

It is advisable to have the dam examined by your veterinarian as soon as practical after delivery, perhaps after she has spent the first quiet day with her family. Hopefully the veterinarian will be able to see the dam and kittens in your home. The experienced fingers of a clinician can determine whether or not all kittens have been delivered. Her mammae may be examined for the presence of abnormalities. An injection of oxytocin (pituitary hormone) may be given to help evacuate the uterus of fluid and placental shreds. Advance arrangements should be made with your veterinarian for this service.

Feeding Kittens

Supplemental feeding of kittens during the first weeks of life is unnecessary if the dam is well and has ample milk, and if the kittens are clean, happy, eating well, and gaining weight. The mother's nutritional requirements continue to increase as her kittens grow. Her caloric intake increased by about 25 percent during gestation, and will increase another 25 percent by the time the kittens are weaned. Those figures are average, not literal. They depend on litter size and the quality of food being fed.

If you wish to monitor the kittens' growth, weigh them individually several times a week to ascertain their rate of gain. Kittens normally weigh between 3 and 4 ounces (86–115 g) at birth. After the first day, they should gain at least 0.5 ounce (14 g) each day. If weighing them, be sure that you check their weights at the same time each day. It is common for a robust kitten to weigh 1 pound (0.5 kg) at one month of age, quadrupling its birth weight in those four weeks.

If kittens do not gain at the expected rate, don't hesitate to supplement their diet with a commercial feline milk replacement formula. It should be fed through one of the nursing devices that is fitted with an appropriate size nipple. Use of a syringe to force-feed tiny kittens may be an acceptable procedure in experienced hands, but it is fraught with dangers when attempted by a novice. If forced feeding is necessary, it is sometimes safer to use a stomach tube. Consult with your veterinarian who can instruct you in the proper technique to force-feed a kitten.

Bengal kittens may be slower than other breeds in their acceptance of solid food. They will begin eating solid food sometime between three and six weeks of age. They should not be forced to do so at a certain age, nor

Male kitten on the right, female on the left.

should they be separated from their mother before she weans them, even if they are eating cat food well.

A good way to start the kittens on solid food is to mix a tablespoonful of a premium, canned kitten formula or strained meat baby food with a similar amount of dry, human baby cereal, and moisten the mixture with feline milk replacer until it reaches the consistency of thick pea soup. Put that mixture in a saucer and dip the kittens' muzzles into it. They will lick it from their whiskers and faces and will usually begin immediately to search for the source of that good stuff. After two or three such training sessions, decrease the milk replacer in the mixture, and increase the cereal and cat food.

Once they have become accustomed to canned food, some premium dry kitten food may be soaked with milk replacer and added to the canned diet in place of the baby cereal. After they

Millwood Patticake *and* Calipurr, *at 12 weeks of age.*

have fully accepted that mixture, begin increasing the amount offered, and feed it twice daily. At that time, make dry kitten food available to them, free choice, and offer them a spoonful or two of canned kitten food twice a day.

When kittens begin to eat solid food, their mother will stop consuming their excretions. It is therefore very important that when you begin supplemental feeding, you also place a couple of litter pans in the nursery. Usually, the mother will use the pans first, and the kittens begin to use them almost immediately.

The Health Status of Kittens

There are several ways to monitor the health status of kittens. It is typical for kittens to lose a bit of weight their first day, but after a day or two of life, kittens should be round, firm, and fully packed. They should have moist

noses, bright pink, moist tongues and lips, and supple skins. Their coats should be clean and well groomed, and they should squirm and wriggle when picked up. They should only cry when the mother steps on them, when they are handled by humans, or when they are rooted away from a nipple by a sibling.

A kitten that cries continuously or frequently for no apparent reason, may be in trouble. It may be injured or have colic or some other illness, but it needs attention. One that appears limp when it is picked up or one with mucus bubbling from its nose or that makes moist sounds when it breathes is not normal.

Consult with your Bengal's veterinarian about your observations. If he or she advises you to take the temperature of the kitten, use a human rectal thermometer, and insert only the well-lubricated bulb into the anus. The new noninvasive thermometers may be useful in monitoring the kittens' temperature as well.

A dry-skinned kitten that feels thin or appears bloated may be in trouble. A kitten that is too weak to compete successfully for a nipple or one that is found by itself, separated from the rest of the litter, should be watched carefully. A kitten that is ignored by the dam needs prompt attention. If the mother does not allow it to nurse, pushes it aside, and does not clean and minister to it, it is likely to be in big trouble.

Tough as kittens are, they have practically no reservoir of strength or nutrition to call upon when they are so young and tiny. It is always advisable to consult with your pet health professional when you suspect illness in a kitten.

The Umbilical Cord: Usually, the umbilical cord requires no attention after it is severed from the placenta. It will dry up and fall off or will be chewed off by the mother within a week or two after birth. If a cord appears swollen and inflamed, the kitten is restless, and the abdomen is tender when touched, call your veterinarian immediately.

Umbilical hernias are very uncommon in kittens, but if they occur they can be recognized as round, soft swellings of the navel. If the umbilical skin has parted, or if any blood or serum is evident, consider it an emergency and call the vet immediately. If the skin is sealed and no tenderness is apparent, you should alert the veterinarian to the situation, but it is probably not an emergency.

The Eyes: Kittens are born with their eyes tightly sealed. They usually open between the eighth and twelfth day of life. Their ear canals are also sealed at birth, and they open a few days after the eyes. Infrequently, a yellow or green discharge exudes from the eyelids of a kitten at about the time the lids separate. If that

Grand champion Millwood Inner Circle, *a female with beautiful rosettes.*

occurs, gently swab both eyes with a cotton ball that has been soaked with ophthalmic boric acid solution obtained from a pharmacy. That treatment should be repeated four or five times a day until no further discharge is seen. If the discharge does not diminish after two days of home treatment, call your veterinarian.

Less common is a tender swelling beneath the eyelids before the eyes open, which may indicate that an infection is trapped under the sealed eyelids. If you wish to try first aid before contacting your veterinarian, wash the eyes with cotton balls soaked in ophthalmic boric acid solution. Gentle, brisk rubbing of the eyelids may cause them to open, and they can then be cleaned as described above. Do not pry or cut the eyelids apart, and if the eyelids do not open with washing, make an early appointment with the kitten's veterinarian.

Nursing Care for Sick Kittens

If forced feeding is necessary for any reason, consult with your veterinarian about the product, the frequency and quantity to feed, and the safest procedure to use.

Heat lamps are dangerous and should not be used to provide warmth for kittens. There are several ways that the proper temperature can be maintained in a sick bed, but sunlamps or infrared lights are not among them.

The best place for a kitten until weaning is with its mother. If she rejects an ill kitten and pushes it from the nest, you must act as her substitute. Groom it frequently with a dry cloth and stimulate its excretions by washing its belly and anal area with the corner of a damp washcloth. Keep it warm, and provide its nutrition.

If the patient is less than two or three weeks old, an incubator may be needed. One can be fashioned from a small box and a heating pad wrapped several times with toweling or flannel cloth. A small cat carrier also makes a good incubator. Before the sick kitten is introduced, adjust the pad's thermostat so that the floor of the incubator stays at 85°F (29.4°C) constantly. Be sure that there is ample floor space that is unheated to which the kitten may escape. Too much heat is as bad as not enough!

Before a rejected kitten is medicated or fed, take its temperature, stimulate excretions, and clean its anal area. Upon the advice of your veterinarian, warm (97 or 98°F [36.1–36.7°C]) dextrose solution may be fed instead of milk replacer if a kitten's body temperature is subnormal.

After the necessary treatment and feeding, place the kitten with its mother. If she accepts it, leave the kitten until the next treatment. If not, return the kitten to the incubator.

The amount of dextrose or milk replacer that is fed depends upon the condition and age of the kitten. In a newborn, about 2 cc of dextrose or milk replacer should be given every two hours. If the kitten nurses from a bottle, do not limit the quantity of milk replacer fed.

Weaning the Litter

After kittens are eating solid food, the mother will instinctively pay less attention to her brood, and she may voluntarily stop nursing them. Your Bengal dam's instincts are phenomenal! If she continues to be possessive of her babies and shows no desire to wean them, let her instincts rule.

When the kittens are separated from their dam, give them free access to a premium dry kitten food and at least two meals of canned kitten food each day. Supply them with a scratching post, clip their toenails, and provide at least one litter pan for every three kittens. An easily cleaned bathroom or a large cat kennel make excellent nurseries.

From about three weeks of age, the kittens are in the most impressionable stage of their lives. That is when they bond to humans readily, and they need human attention on a frequent and regular basis. They should be individually handled several times a day. The more they are petted, groomed, and played with, the better pets they will make as adults.

Selling Kittens

After the litter is weaned and the kittens are eating solid food, it is time to start thinking about sharing the joy of Bengal ownership with the cat loving community. There are several items of business that must be attended to before offering your brood to the public.

Begin the registration process as soon as the litter is born. Ascertain the colors and sexes of your kittens, and send the application for litter registration papers to TICA or the registry of your choice. In response to your registration application, a packet of blue slips will be mailed to you from the registry. Check the sexes and colors listed on the forms to be sure that they match those of the kittens. When the kittens are bestowed upon their new owners, a blue slip will accompany each, unless other arrangements are made, such as might be the case with a mis-marked kitten that you place as a pet. A three-generation pedigree should go with each kitten as well.

Remember all the questions that you asked when you acquired your Bengal, and be prepared to answer them.

Is everyone eating well? To ascertain the appetites of the brood, separate them at feeding time for a day or two. Feed each kitten a couple of teaspoonful of canned food, in separate bowls, in different rooms or parts of the house.

Evaluate the quality of each kitten. Although they have the same genetic makeup, they will differ in value according to their conformity to the breed standard. In this regard, it is best to secure the opinion of an unbiased third party. A Bengal breeder friend or an associate you have met at a cat show will suffice. Perhaps you know a show hall judge who might help.

Consult your veterinarian about a litter examination before the kittens are offered for sale. If possible, have them examined in your home, rather than taking the litter to the animal hospital.

When they are about six weeks of age, an animal health care professional should verify the kittens' good health and freedom from congenital abnormalities. The kittens should be examined for umbilical hernias, congenital heart problems, and other obscure defects. If you intend to keep the kittens until they receive their first vaccination, the exam and vaccinations can be handled at a single visit. You may pay a veterinarian to administer the vaccine or you may elect to do it yourself. In either case, record the brand name, type of vaccine used, and the date given, on a vaccination record for each kitten. On the same record, or independently, the physical examination should be noted.

Age to Sell

As a Bengal breeder, you should observe the kittens daily. With advice from other breeders and your health care specialist, you can determine when each kitten is ready to be placed in a new home. (See The Age of Your New Kitten, page 27).

Meeting Prospective Buyers

If you have been showing the dam, selling the best of her offspring should present no great problem. Word of mouth or a note in your club's newsletter will bring inquiries from interested Bengal breeders. Purebred kittens of lesser quality deserve good homes too. A mis-marked body or less than desirable conformation is no reason to hide a kitten in the closet. Bengals make great pets, even if they can't win show titles.

Pets can be advertised through magazines, newsletters, and newspaper ads. To avoid misunderstandings, be sure to identify the quality of kittens being offered in your ads. When you receive phone call inquiries, make your sale policy known to the caller. If you require that the pet be altered at maturity, or if you plan to withhold pedigree and registration until proof of altering is shown, let the prospective buyer know those restrictions up front. If prices are negotiable, give the potential owner your starting figure and let them know that you might consider a counteroffer.

Remember that you, as a purebred Bengal breeder, have an extended obligation when you sell a kitten. You must back your kittens with certain guarantees. Discuss that subject with other breeders, read newsletter articles from Bengal clubs, or write for advice from established breeders. You

Female leopard.

will probably find that most ethical Bengal breeders will take back any cat they sell if the buyer can no longer care for it. Some may even refund a portion of the purchase price.

When potential buyers of kittens telephone, screen them discreetly. Keep your inquiries circumspect, but discover as much as you can about other pets in their home, how much space is available, how the Bengal will be housed, the buyers' reasons for wanting a Bengal, and their desire and capability to care for the kitten. Ask them not to handle other cats immediately before coming to see your healthy Bengal kittens. Explain that diseases can be transmitted by human vectors. When they arrive, if they have been handling other kittens, provide soap and water and a clean towel. If they understand your motives when making that request, they will appreciate your concern.

Let the buyers watch the kittens from a distance first. Take them to the nursery, or bring the kittens out where they can be observed.

Prospective Bengal owners appreciate knowing what the kittens will look like as an adult. Have the dam and other closely related Bengals present as well. If the sire is not available, show them his picture. Be sure to identify any kittens in the litter that are not for sale. Paint a couple of toenails on kittens that are already spoken for or that you intend to keep.

Show them the pedigree and registration papers of the litter, as well as any contracts or agreements that apply to the sale. Let them see the health and vaccination records, including the need for future vaccinations. Discuss the show and breeding potential of the various kittens offered for sale.

It is very important that prospective buyers understand the cat overpopulation problem. If they are searching for a pet Bengal, impress upon them the need for castration or spaying at the appropriate time. An agreement or contract may be used to further promote altering of pets. Inform them of the hazards of allowing their pet outside, whether altered or not.

Health Care

The health of your cat depends upon many factors, including proper immunization. To vaccinate a kitten and provide it with food and water does not assure its good health. The health or disease status of a cat is affected by physical, emotional, infectious, and nutritional stress factors. Those factors are related to the genetics of the cat, exposure to diseases, the population density of the environment (the number of cats in the household or cattery), the quality and quantity of nutrition provided, exercise provisions, sanitation of the physical environment, and both natural and induced immunity to diseases.

Providing health care for a Bengal is no different from that of any other breed of domestic cats. Bengals have no recognized idiosyncrasies that require special health care considerations.

Many hybrid animals of other species seem to enjoy a certain degree of hybrid vigor. That term is used to describe a phenomenon wherein the offspring of parents of two different species possess a greater strength or resistance to disease than either parent. Bengals of the F-1 generation are reported by many owners and breeders to be extremely disease-resistant, hardy animals. Whether Bengals of the fourth generation and beyond express hybrid vigor is only conjecture.

There is reason to believe that the Asian leopard cat is resistant to feline leukemia virus (FeLV), which causes a very serious disease in domestic cats.

Ten-month-old male with nice rosettes, playing in water.

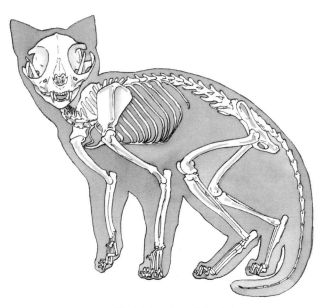

Skeletal system of the feline.

ally considered to be safer to use, especially in very young and very old animals. They are probably inferior to the live vaccines in terms of protection because they do not replicate in the vaccinated animal's tissues and the immune response is slower and less complete.

Other vaccines are made from microscopic pathogenic organisms (primarily viruses), that have been treated in some way to modify or attenuate them. Modification allows the infectious agent to remain alive, and when it is introduced into a healthy animal it replicates in the tissues of that animal, but it is unable to cause disease. Those are modified live-virus (MLV) vaccines, and they are generally considered to confer more reliable immunity than killed-virus vaccines. Replicating vaccine viruses may be shed from the vaccinated animals (see The Bengal Vaccine Controversy, following).

Recent technical advances involve the preparation of vaccines from particles of viruses. Fragments of a virus are split away from the disease-causing organism. When administered to a healthy animal, they stimulate an immune response in the vaccinated animal, but it is impossible for the fragments to cause disease.

How a Vaccine Works

The administration of a vaccine is intended to stimulate a dynamic, ongoing process called an immune response. That response involves the production of white blood cells and antibodies that attack and destroy invading pathogens before they can cause disease. Immune response includes the establishment of a memory process (anamnesis) that hastens the response to future exposures to the infectious agent.

The level of immunity that develops from a vaccination is dependent upon

One might speculate that some of that resistance may be inherited by domestic Bengals, but no documented proof of such resistance has been published.

Vaccinations for various diseases are important to maintain your Bengal's good health. The rapidly developing field of biotechnology introduces new immunizing agents annually. A disease may be endemic in some parts of the country, and totally absent in others. That fact alone makes a general schedule nearly worthless. Your Bengal's specific vaccination schedule should originate with your local veterinarian.

Vaccines

Vaccines are agents that, when administered properly to a healthy animal, cause that animal to develop immunity to a disease. Some vaccines are prepared from killed bacteria, viruses, or other microscopic pathogens (disease-causing organisms). Those killed products are usu-

the cat's health, its age, its existing passive immunity, its prior vaccination history, and past exposure to the pathogen. The degree or quality of immunity conferred by a vaccine is also related to the particular infectious agent involved, its antigenicity, the vaccine concentration, and the route of vaccine administration.

When a cat has some degree of immunity to a disease, and is subsequently vaccinated for that disease, its immunity will normally be boosted. Without boosters or exposure to the disease, its immunity gradually decreases.

It is important that booster vaccinations are given to stimulate and maintain the anamnestic (memory) response in a vaccinated animal. Vaccines are not perfect.

A strong, healthy cat will resist disease by virtue of its good health. A healthy, active cat will respond well to vaccinations and will develop more complete immunity to disease. Vaccinations given to cats suffering from poor nutrition, disease, or other stresses may be a waste of good biologics and may give owners a false sense of security.

The Bengal Vaccine Controversy

There is an ongoing debate about the types of vaccines that should be used in Bengals. Some breeders believe that only killed-virus vaccines should be used, because the safety and effectiveness of modified-live virus (MLV) vaccines have not been proven in wild animals.

Because Bengal house pets are four or more generations removed from their wild ancestors, most health care professionals treat Bengals exactly the same as other domestic breeds. It is important to remember that Bengals are house cats, not wild animals.

There is a potential (if remote) threat that a virus contained in an

Muscular system of the feline.

MLV vaccine might revert to a disease-causing state. I have found no documentation indicating that any of the current MLV viruses have ever reverted to a virulent state and caused a disease in domestic felines.

Virus shedding may occur with MLV vaccines. The shedding is related to the fact that the MLV virus replicates in the tissues of the vaccinated animal. A shed virus is not necessarily virulent (capable of causing disease).

There are reports of virus shed from vaccinated domestic cats causing symptoms in wild cats that are housed near the vaccinated domestic cats. If you keep wild cats, your vaccination program should be discussed with health care professionals who have experience with vaccines used in those animals.

Most commonly used pet drugs and biologics have *not* been extensively researched in wild animals. The fact

What a lovely red chair; I think I'll keep it.

those vaccines and they trust MLV vaccines to confer good immunity to the animals on which they are used.

The U.S. Department of Agriculture, Biologics Section, advises that there are no federal regulations that govern the use of MLV vaccines on hybrid outcrosses from the Asian leopard cat and the domestic cat. Their policy is to leave the administration of any biologic to the discretion of licensed veterinarians.

Representatives of three major companies that research, license, produce, and distribute feline vaccines were contacted. They agreed that there is no research data to support their opinions, but their products are assumed to be safe and efficacious for use in domestic Bengal cats. None were aware of any adverse reactions to their products when used in domestic Bengal cats, hybrids, or wild animals.

Many veterinarians who specialize in feline medicine use killed-virus vaccines in exotic felines such as the lynx and Asian leopard cats. Bengals are treated the same as any other domestic cat in virtually every way. If a particular vaccine or therapeutic agent is not considered efficacious or safe for use in other house cats, it will not be used in Bengals. Products used in other cats are also used in Bengals.

That any individual of any breed may suffer an adverse reaction to a drug or biologic is a calculated risk taken by veterinarians and cat owners every day. It is not a peculiar risk in Bengal cats. The use of particular drugs or vaccines is left to the discretion of the animals' owners and their veterinarians.

Infectious Diseases

Rabies: A lethal disease of all mammals, rabies is transmitted by direct contact with the saliva of an infected animal. It is therefore rarely a threat to house cats and another

that a product is safe and efficacious in one species does not necessarily mean that it is dangerous or ineffective when used in other animals, but there is always a question.

A majority of the veterinary practitioners that I contacted, who have occasion to vaccinate *wild* felines, use killed vaccines when available. Those who administer MLV vaccines did not report adverse reactions to

good reason to keep your Bengal in your house. Rabies vaccination requirements vary from place to place according to local ordinances and in at least 12 states' statutes. Consult with your veterinarian about the age at which your cat should be vaccinated, as well as the need for booster vaccinations.

The most common reservoirs of infection for rabies virus are raccoons, bats, skunks, and other wild mammals. All rabies vaccines currently in use are killed-virus products.

Healthy cats may be vaccinated initially between three and six months of age, then again when a year old. A booster may be given every one to three years, depending upon the particular vaccine used and the laws that apply.

Feline leukemia virus (FeLV): This virus causes a complex, often fatal disease in cats that may be manifested in many different ways. It may suppress the cat's immune system and cause severe anemia, and it is frequently associated with cancer of the lungs and kidneys. Often, the only outwardly visible symptoms are gradual health degeneration, weight loss, lethargy, and depression.

FeLV can be contracted through bite wounds and other contact routes, or it can be transmitted from mother to kittens before or at the time of birth. Blood tests can detect FeLV, but the interpretation and significance of test results are controversial in the health care community at this time. FeLV tests and vaccination programs vary from one area of the country to another, and from year to year, as new research results are published and new biologic products are developed. Because FeLV is so unpredictable, your health care professional should be consulted before vaccinating.

Feline panleukopenia virus (FPV): Also called cat distemper or feline enteritis, FPV is one of the most common and severe viral diseases of cats. It is especially lethal in young kittens, but it can cause death in cats of all ages. In the very young, there may be few identifiable symptoms. The kitten may appear normal one moment and become lethargic and limp a few hours later. Within a few more hours, the infected kitten may be comatose or even dead. In older cats, the symptoms usually include severe diarrhea, vomiting, and dehydration.

A series of vaccinations against panleukopenia is recommended for all kittens, beginning by eight to ten weeks of age, depending on the circumstances. Annual booster vaccinations are essential.

Feline viral rhinotracheitis (FVR): One of several upper respiratory diseases of cats, FVR is typically manifested by sneezing, purulent ocular and nasal discharge, and redness of the membranes of the eyes. Cats affected with this disease often dehydrate rapidly, and frequently they have no appetite. Those complications make the disease noteworthy in all ages, but especially in the young. Rhinotracheitis may be accompanied by pneumonia, which can be fatal.

FVR is spread by aerosol (sneeze) contact from infected cats. It is most prevalent in outdoor cats or in animals that come into contact with infected cats in boarding kennels or cat shows. House cats can contract the disease from infected cats through open, screened windows.

Vaccination is recommended for all cats. The vaccine is often packaged in combination with other vaccines.

Feline calici virus (FCV): This virus causes erosions on the tongue, lips, gums, nostrils, throat, and sometimes eyelid membranes. It is often complicated by a reduced appetite and dehydration. It usually runs a relatively short course, and is rarely fatal.

Stages of illness in kittens.

The secondary appetite loss and dehydration problems can be very serious, and the infection reduces the animal's resistance to other diseases. It often accompanies rhinotracheitis, and is also spread by aerosol.

Vaccinations are recommended for all cats, using the same schedule as FVR and FPV vaccinations.

Feline chlamydiosis (pneumonitis): A disease that is manifested by sneezing and inflammation of the membranes of the nostrils and the eyes, feline chlamydiosis is caused by the Chlamydia organism that is neither a virus nor a bacterium. The infection produces symptoms similar to FCV and FVR. It is highly conta-gious and may occur in cattery situations as a neonatal disease. It is treatable and is thus less dangerous than FCV or FVR. Unfortunately, all three of those diseases may infect a cat concurrently.

Chlamydia vaccine is a killed product that is frequently combined with the vaccines for FPV, FCV, and FVR. The same vaccination schedule may be used.

Vaccines for the upper respiratory diseases discussed above are usually protective, however they are not 100 percent effective under all circumstances. Booster vaccinations are very important.

Feline infectious peritonitis (FIP): A lethal viral disease of cats, FIP symptoms in the early stages include a persistent fever, but other signs are very obscure. Later, infected cats may suffer from abdominal or chest fluid production. There is no known successful treatment for the disease. It does not occur as frequently as the other feline diseases discussed, and is not as well understood as most other cat diseases.

A vaccine is available, but veterinarians often recommend FIP vaccination only in high-risk situations.

Noncontagious Diseases

Feline urological syndrome (FUS): In a class by itself, FUS claims the lives of thousands of adult male cats annually. In current literature, the syndrome is called feline lower urinary tract disease (FLUTD). Until the advent of new, carefully balanced commercial diets for cats, FUS was one of the most common, potentially fatal disease syndromes seen in male cats.

FUS is a blockage of the urethra of male cats caused by mucus plugs and tiny sandlike stones (struvite crystals) that originate in the bladder. Within hours after total obstruction, the cat begins to suffer intense abdominal pain, and if not treated very early, the cat will absorb toxic waste products from his urine. Kidney degeneration and uremic poisoning follow, and the cat will die.

The mucus and crystal formation probably occurs in many female cats as well, but due to the anatomical differences between the male and female, only the male's life is frequently at risk. A male cat's urethra bends around the pelvic bone, then it narrows as it passes through the penis. Solid and semisolid particles collect in that curved funnel, and an obstruction is formed. The shorter, wider, more elastic urethra of the female allows mucus and "sand" to pass without obstructing urine flow.

FUS is a medical emergency! If symptoms are observed, your veterinarian should be called immediately.

Initially, an affected cat makes frequent trips to his litter pan. He strains for a few seconds, then leaves the pan, only to return a short while later and repeat the process. He licks his penis and perineal area frequently. When you check the litter to see if any urine has been passed, you may see no urine, or perhaps only a few drops, with a drop or two of blood.

As the condition progresses, he squats in the litter box in a urinating or defecating position for extended periods of time, and often cries in pain. By that time, he will be totally disinterested in food and water. Later, he will appear disoriented and glassy eyed. He will lie on his side and cry in pain when he is touched.

Cats sometimes give their owners early warning that they have urinary disease. They will jump into a sink, or onto a countertop or table, and urinate. Often the urine will contain a few drops of blood mixed with the urine. If that is observed, take the cat to your veterinarian before other symptoms develop.

FUS is seen in all breeds of cats in all parts of the country. It is not as

Third eyelids pulled up are a sign of illness.

common today as it was in the past, but if it should occur, your male cat's life may depend upon early detection of FUS symptoms and immediate veterinary treatment.

Hair ball (trichobezoar): The formation of hair balls in the stomach and intestines of cats is a common condition. As a cat grooms itself, it swallows the hair that is pulled out with its tongue. Hair is nearly indigestible, and it often forms tightly woven mats in the stomach or upper small intestine that must be passed in the feces or vomited. A cat with hair balls may have a persistent dry cough and reduced appetite shortly before vomiting a mouse-shaped hair ball. Treatment, if required, usually employs the regular use of lubricants that may be added to the cat's food.

Gingivitis: An infection of the gums, gingivitis is usually associated with dental problems such as heavy tartar on your cat's teeth. The signs usually observed include bad breath

Triple grand champion Gogees Thunderbolt, *one-year-old muscular male.*

and a reluctance to pick up or chew solid food. It is a condition seen primarily in middle-aged or older cats. Treatment is usually begun by cleaning the teeth and removing the tartar. In advanced cases, a tooth or several teeth may require extraction.

Otitis externa: This infection of the outer ear canal may be related to an infestation of ear mites (which are contagious), excessive wax buildup in the ear canal, or the presence of foreign material. The cat may scratch at an ear and hold it tipped downward. You may observe a foul-smelling discharge from the ear. Treatment usually includes thorough cleaning of the ear canals, and possibly the use of drops in the ear, oral antibiotics, or a combination thereof.

Wounds and abscesses: Common in outdoor cats, especially in toms, abscesses are usually the result of cat fight puncture wounds that are not treated immediately or adequately. Treatment of wounds or abscesses

depends upon the location and state of the infection. Prevention is easier, cheaper, and safer than treatment! Keep your Bengal in the house.

Skin Diseases

Ringworm: A contagious fungal disease of the skin that is especially prevalent in cats, ringworm is more commonly seen in cats that are under stress from overcrowding, lack of exercise, poor nutrition, or an unclean environment. In an acute, clinical infection, skin lesions are raised, inflamed, hairless circles on the skin. Subclinical ringworm is much more common, and is manifested by scaling of the skin, broken hair shafts, and only slight hair loss.

Animals with subclinical infections may act as carriers or reservoirs of infection for other cats, other household pets, and sometimes humans. It can be transmitted by handling an infected animal, then handling a susceptible animal.

Eight-month-old tricolored marble male.

Specific diagnosis is made in a clinical laboratory. Treatment varies according to the circumstances. It may be necessary to use oral medication, topical medication, medicated baths, or a combination of techniques.

Mange: A less commonly diagnosed skin disease of cats, mange may be caused by any of several skin mites including Demodex, the Notoedric mite, or Cheyletiella.

Diagnosis is made in the laboratory and treatment is managed by specific drugs applied to the skin. Mange is often related to stress factors, and some health professionals recommend vitamin therapy and nutritional improvement in addition to the prescribed therapeutic products.

Flea bite allergy: Causing intensive itching, especially in the area of the base of the tail and along the flanks, this dermatitis is an allergy to the saliva of the flea. Obviously, the diagnosis depends upon finding fleas or the excreta of fleas on the cat, and the treatment is to rid the cat of the flea infestation.

Diet hypersensitivity: Not common, but occasionally seen in all animals, diet hypersensitivity symptoms are generalized pruritus (itching) over most of the body. After ruling out more common causes of skin irritation, diet changes may be prescribed to ascertain which ingredient in the Bengal's diet is causing the problem. Fortunately, there are now foods available that make both diagnosis and treatment of allergies easier.

Internal Parasites

There are a number of internal parasites that may infest your Bengal. Some of those parasites can be passed to kittens from an infested dam at or shortly after birth. Infestations may be the result of exposure to the parasite eggs or larvae that are shed from other infested cats as well. Not all worms or other parasites are large enough to see with the naked eye, and diagnosis is made in a laboratory.

Tapeworms: Two-host parasites, tapeworms are found in cats that kill and eat certain small rodents, or in

those that are infested with fleas. Either fleas or rodents may be secondary hosts for tapeworms. If cats ingest infested fleas or rodents, the adult form of the tapeworm will develop in the intestines of the cats. Tapeworms are segmented, thin, flat parasites that grow to great lengths in cats' intestinal tracts. As the worms mature, small segments drop off and may be found in infested cats' feces or stuck to the hair around their anus. Dry tapeworm segments look like tiny grains of rice. Finding those segments is diagnostic for tapeworms.

Toxoplasma coccidial **infestation:** Although rare, this parasite has public health significance and should be discussed with your veterinarian, whether or not it is suspected in your cat.

Isospora: Coccidia that are much more common in cats, *isospora* may cause chronic diarrhea and weight loss in young kittens, and are seen more frequently in outdoor cats.

Roundworms: Nematodes such as *Toxocara cati* have a complex life cycle in cats. They are known to infest kittens at an early age through infested mothers' milk. Skinny, inactive kittens should be suspected of being infested. Breeding queens should have a fecal examination done before they are bred to assure that they are not infested.

Hookworms *(Ancylostoma):* Infestations of hookworms are rare in the United States, but when they occur, they are significant because they may cause intestinal bleeding. A thin, inactive, weak or anemic appearing kitten may possibly be infested.

Diagnosis of the above and other internal parasites is usually made through microscopic examinations of the feces of your pet. A fresh fecal sample from your new Bengal should be taken to your veterinarian for laboratory examination.

Hormonal Imbalances

Hyperthyroidism: A hormonal imbalance that is occasionally seen in middle-aged and older cats, hyperthyroidism exhibits such symptoms as weight loss, increased appetite accompanied by voluminous stool production, restlessness, excitability, and increased shedding. It is diagnosed by laboratory blood tests.

Hyperadrenocortism: Another uncommon hormonal disease that sometimes accompanies diabetes, hyperadrenocortism displays such symptoms as a potbelly and increased water intake with concurrent increased urination. It is usually seen in older cats and it is especially prevalent in cats that have received steroid (cortisone) therapy.

Diabetes mellitus: Another disease of older cats, this hormonal imbalance has symptoms similar to those discussed immediately above. All of the above diseases are very complex and are diagnosed only by laboratory tests.

Poisoning (Toxicosis)

Outdoor cats are more likely to be poisoned than indoor pets. Cats' grooming habits often get them in trouble with poisons. They lick their feet clean, no matter what they may have stepped in.

If they get an insecticide on their feet, they may be poisoned. Boric acid is only mildly toxic, causing diarrhea and excessive salivation. Rotenone is generally considered nontoxic but if ingested by a cat, it may cause lethargy. Keep cleaning and disinfecting agents out of the reach of cats.

Certain houseplants may poison cats. If your pet munches on your plants, consult your veterinarian about the possible dangers from the specific vegetation that your Bengal enjoys.

Human drugs such as aspirin, ibuprofens, acetaminophens, antihistamines, and some antibiotics can be dangerous when ingested by cats.

Metabolic Diseases of Older Cats

Senile cataracts: The result of aging of the lens of the eyes, cataracts rarely cause total blindness. The normally soft, gelatinous lens material becomes hardened and opaque and appears as a white or blue structure behind the iris. The cats' other senses usually remain sharp enough to compensate for the loss of visual acuity.

Osteoarthritis: This is an old cat disease that causes swelling and loss of normal function of the joints of the body. The pain resulting from arthritis can sometimes be reduced with medication. Do not attempt home therapy. Aspirin and several other human anti-inflammatory drugs are toxic to cats unless the dosage is calculated carefully.

Deafness: Observed in a few very old cats, deafness is a degenerative condition for which there is rarely any treatment, but the patients seem oblivious to their loss of hearing. Owners and deaf house pets find ways to communicate through touch and manage quite nicely.

Kidney failure: This degenerative disease claims many lives. Aged animals compensate for a gradual loss of kidney function by drinking increasing amounts of water. When they are unable to consume and eliminate sufficient quantities of water, they become uremic. If kidney compromise is discovered early, special diets are available to reduce the stress on those organs. When your old Bengal's thirst increases, and it is observed making frequent trips to the litter box, consult your veterinarian.

Congenital Deformities

Congenital anatomical deformities of Bengals are those that are present at birth. Some are hereditary, others are possibly genetically transmitted, but not enough data is available to be sure. The few congenital physical deformities that have been reported are not unique to Bengals.

To protect the Bengal's future, students of the breed generally agree that repeated breeding of the parents of congenitally deformed offspring should be discouraged except under exceptional and controlled research conditions. Similarly, normal appearing siblings of a congenitally deformed kitten are usually placed as pets to be altered at maturity.

Chest compression: Occasionally, a kitten with chest compression (swimmer kitten) shows up in a Bengal litter. It is not limited to Bengals, and it does not appear to be a threat to the Bengal breed. The condition is manifested by ventro-dorsal chest compression. (Its thorax is flattened between the spine and sternum.)

It is also known by the human anatomical term *Pectus excavatum*, and is generally considered to be genetically transmitted in cats. It is believed by some to be associated with nutrition of the dam, and it may be a combination of both. It is seen in varying degrees of severity.

If you acquire a kitten that you suspect has chest compression, the breeder should be notified and your veterinarian should be consulted immediately for diagnosis and prognosis.

The parents of chest compression kittens should be removed from the breeding program because the condition is assumed to be genetically transmitted until proven otherwise.

Patellar (kneecap) displacement: Another congenital deformity that has been reported in Bengals and other breeds, kneecap displacement is assumed to be genetically transmitted as well. The condition is not life-threat-

Keep your cat indoors.

ening, and can usually be surgically repaired, giving a normal life to the affected pet. Affected cats shouldn't be used in a breeding program.

Congenital hip dysplasia: This deformity has been diagnosed in a few breeds, including Bengals. More information on hip dysplasia is available in the canine, where it is known to be hereditary. If the same holds true in cats, affected animals should not be used for breeding.

Other congenital deformities of cats include crooked tails and crossed eyes, as well as other ocular problems. Hair and coat peculiarities, extra toes, and other physical anomalies may occur as well. Many are believed to be genetically transmitted. If you suspect that a kitten may not be entirely normal, the breeder of the kitten should be notified immediately, and if a second opinion is desired, your veterinarian should be consulted.

Giving Your Bengal a Pill

Fortunately, many feline drugs are now packaged in flavored, liquid formulations and dropper bottles, but it is sometimes necessary to give your kitten a pill. Consider the following technique.

First, put about one-half teaspoonful of butter or margarine in a saucer, near the pill, on a countertop. Wrap your Bengal in a large towel, with only its head protruding from the towel cocoon. Place your left hand (assuming that you are right-handed), palm

Giving a pill to your Bengal.

Supreme grand champion Heritage Kimo *displays desirable body type and coat pattern.*

down on top of the cat's head. Then grip its head with the tip of your thumb on the right cheek, and your index or middle finger on the left. Press the tips of your finger and thumb inward, forcing the cat's upper lips between its upper and lower rear molar teeth. As you squeeze the lips inward, tip the cat's head back, so that its nose points toward the ceiling, over its back.

When that position is reached, the lower jaw will open. Drop the pill over the top of the tongue, directly into the throat. Immediately relax your grip on your patient's head, and as you do so, dip your right index finger in the butter and wipe it on the nostrils of the patient. The cat will quickly lick its nose to clear the nostrils. In doing so, its tongue comes forward, the cat swallows, and the pill is on its way to the stomach.

Symptoms of Illnesses

Changes in their pets' attitudes, appetites, and habits alert Bengal owners to illnesses. Sometimes it is difficult for pet owners to convey those observed changes to their veterinari-ans in meaningful terms.

Think carefully about the duration of the symptoms that you have observed. They may be associated with some events in the pet's life. For instance, did they begin a few days after the cat was boarded, follow a change in diet, or start after it consumed a house-plant? Make notes of your observations and use them when you call your veterinarian for advice.

A number of symptoms may be present; be sure to record all that you observe. Listed below are some general symptoms, that will help you provide a useful history for your veterinarian.

• **Temperature elevation:** Anytime you suspect illness in your pet, take its temperature. The normal rectal temperature of a cat is between 101 and 102°F (38.3–38.9°C).

• **Not walking:** Can't get up? Tries to rise, falls? Difficulty walking? Staggering? Lame on one leg?

• **Swelling:** Where and how big? Tender when touched? Scab on it? Drainage from it?

Life cycle of the tapeworm.

• **Loss of appetite:** No interest? Eats one food, not another? Refuses all food? Tries to eat, can't? Salivates when eating?

• **Urinary difficulty:** Strains in box? Passes no urine? Urinates in strange places? Bloody, dark brown? Foul odor? Large quantities? Sprays urine?

• **Water intake:** Great quantities? Drinking no water? Drinks then vomits?

• **Defecation:** Constipated? Diarrhea? Loss of control? Color of feces? Feces brittle or hard? Foreign material? Blood or mucus? Cries when defecating?

• **Vomiting:** What is vomited—Parasites? Food? Mucus? Hair mats? When does it occur? How frequently? Follow coughing?

• **Respiration:** Relaxed, smooth? Labored and deep? Raspy sounds? Panting? Sneezing? Coughing?

• **Mucous membrane color:** Gums pale, white? Gums dark red? Blue-tinged?

• **Skin condition:** Hairless patches? Red, inflamed? Itchy? Hair brittle? Dry? General thinning? Scabs? Blood oozing?

• **Attitude:** Grouchy? Super-affectionate? Hides from family? Sits instead of standing?

• **Eyes:** Pupils seem dilated? Pinpoint pupils? Discharge from eyes? Membranes red? Watery, squinting?

• **Weight and Condition:** Weight loss or gain? Obese or very thin?

Don't attempt to diagnose and treat your Bengal based on the numerous illnesses and their symptoms that have been discussed. This information is important for you to be aware of various cat diseases and their symptoms to enable you to convey your observations to your Bengal's veterinarian.

Euthanasia

It is normal for pet owners to refuse to entertain thoughts of the inevitable loss of their pets. Your new Bengal kitten will live for many years, but eventually the end will come. Hopefully it will be quick and painless for both pet and owner. In certain prolonged disease conditions, such as inoperable cancer that does not respond to therapy, you may consider euthanasia. Life and death decisions must be made by owners with the guidance of animal health care professionals. Euthanasia of a pet, in the hands of an experienced professional, can be a quiet, painless, and comfortable way to end a life.

Useful Addresses and Literature

Cat Associations

The International Cat Association Inc.
(TICA)
P.O. Box 2684
Harlingen, Texas 78551
(210) 428-8046
TICA maintains a registry for Bengals. Breed standards for Bengals are maintained and published by TICA, and judges are trained and licensed by that association. Bengals may compete for championship titles in over 250 all-breed TICA cat shows in the United States each year. Another 70 or 80 shows are sponsored by TICA in other nations.

Cat Fanciers Federation (CFF)
9509 Montgomery Road
Cincinnati, Ohio 45242
(513) 984-1841
CFF registers and accepts Bengals for showing in the Provisional Breed Category, together with Siberian and Ocicat. Animals shown in the provisional category cannot earn championship titles. Winning in the provisional category earns points toward the Parade of Perfection, an annual award for the best of the provisional breeds. CFF does not register the Asian leopard cat or any other Bengal foundation stock generations. In order to qualify for CFF registration and showing, the Bengal must be of no less than the fourth generation removed from the Asian leopard cat.

American Cat Fanciers Association
(ACFA)
P.O. Box 203
Point Lookout, Missouri 65726
(417) 334-5430
In the past, ACFA registered Bengals of the F-4 generation and beyond. For a period of time, ACFA accepted them for showing in the New Breed and Color class. That privilege was withdrawn a few years ago. The association still maintains a Bengal registry for those breeders who wish to build the pedigrees of their cats in the ACFA registry.

Cat Fanciers' Association Inc. (CFA)
1805 Atlantic Avenue
P.O. Box 1005
Manasquan, New Jersey 08760
(908) 528-9797
At this time, CFA does not register Bengals and does not allow them to be exhibited in the show hall. Those restrictions are based upon the Bengal's feral genes.

American Cat Association (ACA)
8101 Katherine Avenue
Panorama City, California 91402
(818) 781-5656
The ACA does not register Bengals due to the Asian leopard cat genes that it carries.

Canadian Cat Association
83 Kennedy Road South, Unit 1805
Brampton, Ontario, Canada L6W 3P3
(905) 459-1481

Bengal Breed Clubs

The International Bengal Cat Society (TIBCS)
P.O. Box 403
Powell, Ohio 43065-0403

TIBCS was the first U.S. Bengal breed club or association. It is still the largest, boasting some 400 members. TIBCS publishes a bimonthly newsletter called the *Bengal Bulletin* with members' ads listing kittens for sale. For information write to TIBCS.

Authentic Bengal Cat Club (ABC)
P.O. Box 1653
Roseburg, Oregon 97470

The ABC also publishes a bimonthly newsletter with "kittens for sale" ads.

Cat Magazines

Many periodicals carry information about cats and the cat fancy. At least five cat magazines are found in most pet supply stores and newsstands. Ads for Bengals may be found in all of them.

Cat Fancy
P.O. Box 52864
Boulder, Colorado 80322-2864
(303) 786-7306

Cats U.S.A.
P.O. Box 55811
Boulder, Colorado 80322-5811
(303) 786-7652

I Love Cats
Grass Roots Publishing Company
950 Third Avenue
New York, New York 10022

Cat World International
P.O. Box 35635
Phoenix, Arizona 85069-5635

Cats
2750-A South Ridgewood Ave.
South Daytona, Florida 32119

Index

BARRON'S PET REFERENCE BOOKS

Barron's Pet Reference Books are and have long been the choice of experts and discerning pet owners. Why? Here are just a few reasons. These indispensable volumes are packed with 35 to 200 stunning full-color photos. Each provides the very latest expert information and answers questions that pet owners often wonder about.

BARRON'S PET REFERENCE BOOKS ARE:

AQUARIUM FISH
AQUARIUM FISH BREEDING
THE AQUARIUM FISH SURVIVAL MANUAL
AQUARIUM PLANTS MANUAL
BEFORE YOU BUY THAT KITTEN
BEFORE YOU BUY THAT PUPPY
THE BEST PET NAME BOOK EVER
CARING FOR YOUR OLDER CAT
CARING FOR YOUR OLDER DOG
CARING FOR YOUR SICK CAT
THE CAT CARE MANUAL
CIVILIZING YOUR PUPPY
COMMUNICATING WITH YOUR DOG
THE COMPLETE BOOK OF CAT CARE
THE COMPLETE BOOK OF DOG CARE
THE COMPLETE BOOK OF PARAKEET CARE
THE DOG CARE MANUAL
EDUCATING YOUR DOG
THE EXOTIC PET SURVIVAL MANUAL
FEEDING YOUR PET BIRD
FUN AND GAMES WITH YOUR DOG

GOLDFISH AND ORNAMENTAL CARP
GUIDE TO A WELL-BEHAVED CAT
GUIDE TO A WELL-BEHAVED PARROT
GUIDE TO HOME PET GROOMING
HAND-FEEDING AND RAISING BABY BIRDS
HEALTHY CAT, HAPPY CAT
HEALTHY DOG, HAPPY DOG
HOP TO IT: A Guide To Training Your Pet Rabbit
THE HORSE CARE MANUAL
HOW TO TEACH YOUR OLD DOG NEW TRICKS
INDOOR CATS
LABYRINTH FISH
LIZARD CARE FROM A TO Z
NONVENOMOUS SNAKES
101 QUESTIONS YOUR CAT WOULD ASK
101 QUESTIONS YOUR DOG WOULD ASK
THE SECRET LIFE OF CATS
SHOW ME
THE ULTRAFIT OLDER CAT
THE TROPICAL MARINE FISH SURVIVAL MANUAL
. . . AND MANY MORE

Perfect for Pet Owners!

PET OWNER'S MANUALS

Over 50 illustrations per book (20 or more color photos), 72–80 pp., paperback.

ABYSSINIAN CATS
AFRICAN GRAY PARROTS
AMAZON PARROTS
BANTAMS
BEAGLES
BEEKEEPING
BOSTON TERRIERS
BOXERS
CANARIES
CATS
CHINCHILLAS
CHOW-CHOWS
CICHLIDS
COCKATIELS
COCKER SPANIELS
COCKATOOS
COLLIES
CONURES
DACHSHUNDS
DALMATIANS
DISCUS FISH
DOBERMAN PINSCHERS
DOGS
DOVES
DWARF RABBITS
ENGLISH SPRINGER SPANIELS
FEEDING AND SHELTERING BACKYARD BIRDS
FEEDING AND SHELTERING EUROPEAN BIRDS
FERRETS
GERBILS
GERMAN SHEPHERDS
GOLDEN RETRIEVERS
GOLDFISH
GOULDIAN FINCHES
GREAT DANES
GUINEA PIGS
GUPPIES, MOLLIES, AND PLATTIES
HAMSTERS
HEDGEHOGS
IRISH SETTERS
KEESHONDEN
KILLIFISH
LABRADOR RETRIEVERS
LHASA APSOS
LIZARDS IN THE TERRARIUM
LONGHAIRED CATS

LONG-TAILED PARAKEETS
LORIES AND LORIKEETS
LOVEBIRDS
MACAWS
MICE
MUTTS
MYNAHS
PARAKEETS
PARROTS
PERSIAN CATS
PIGEONS
POMERANIANS
PONIES
POODLES
POT BELLIES AND OTHER MINIATURE PIGS
PUGS
RABBITS
RATS
ROTTWEILERS
SCHNAUZERS
SCOTTISH FOLD CATS
SHAR-PEI
SHEEP
SHETLAND SHEEPDOGS
SHIH TZUS
SIAMESE CATS
SIBERIAN HUSKIES
SMALL DOGS
SNAKES
SPANIELS
TROPICAL FISH
TURTLES
WEST HIGHLAND WHITE TERRIERS
YORKSHIRE TERRIERS
ZEBRA FINCHES

NEW PET HANDBOOKS

Detailed, illustrated profiles (40–60 color photos), 144 pp., paperback.

NEW AQUARIUM FISH HANDBOOK
NEW AUSTRALIAN PARAKEET HANDBOOK
NEW BIRD HANDBOOK
NEW CANARY HANDBOOK
NEW CAT HANDBOOK
NEW COCKATIEL HANDBOOK
NEW DOG HANDBOOK
NEW DUCK HANDBOOK
NEW FINCH HANDBOOK

NEW GOAT HANDBOOK
NEW PARAKEET HANDBOOK
NEW PARROT HANDBOOK
NEW RABBIT HANDBOOK
NEW SALTWATER AQUARIUM HANDBOOK
NEW SOFTBILL HANDBOOK
NEW TERRIER HANDBOOK

REFERENCE BOOKS

Comprehensive, lavishly illustrated references (60–300 color photos), 136–176 pp., hardcover & paperback.

AQUARIUM FISH
AQUARIUM FISH BREEDING
AQUARIUM FISH SURVIVAL MANUAL
AQUARIUM PLANTS MANUAL
BEFORE YOU BUY THAT PUPPY
BEST PET NAME BOOK EVER, THE
CARING FOR YOUR SICK CAT
CAT CARE MANUAL
CIVILIZING YOUR PUPPY
COMMUNICATING WITH YOUR DOG
COMPLETE BOOK OF BUDGERIGARS
COMPLETE BOOK OF CAT CARE
COMPLETE BOOK OF DOG CARE
DOG CARE MANUAL
FEEDING YOUR PET BIRD
GOLDFISH AND ORNAMENTAL CARP
GUIDE TO A WELL-BEHAVED CAT
GUIDE TO HOME PET GROOMING
HEALTHY CAT, HAPPY CAT
HEALTHY DOG, HAPPY DOG
HOP TO IT: A Guide to Training Your Pet Rabbit
HORSE CARE MANUAL
HOW TO TALK TO YOUR CAT
HOW TO TEACH YOUR OLD DOG NEW TRICKS
LABYRINTH FISH
NONVENOMOUS SNAKES
TROPICAL MARINE FISH SURVIVAL MANUAL

Barron's Educational Series, Inc. • 250 Wireless Blvd., Hauppauge, NY 11788
Call toll-free: 1-800-645-3476 • In Canada: Georgetown Book Warehouse
34 Armstrong Ave., Georgetown, Ont. L7G 4R9 • Call toll-free: 1-800-247-7160
Order from your favorite book or pet store.
Visit our web site at: **www.barronseduc.com**

(#62) R 3/99